# Vegetables

## ANTONIO CARLUCCIO

photography by Laura Edwards

quadrille

# CONTENTS

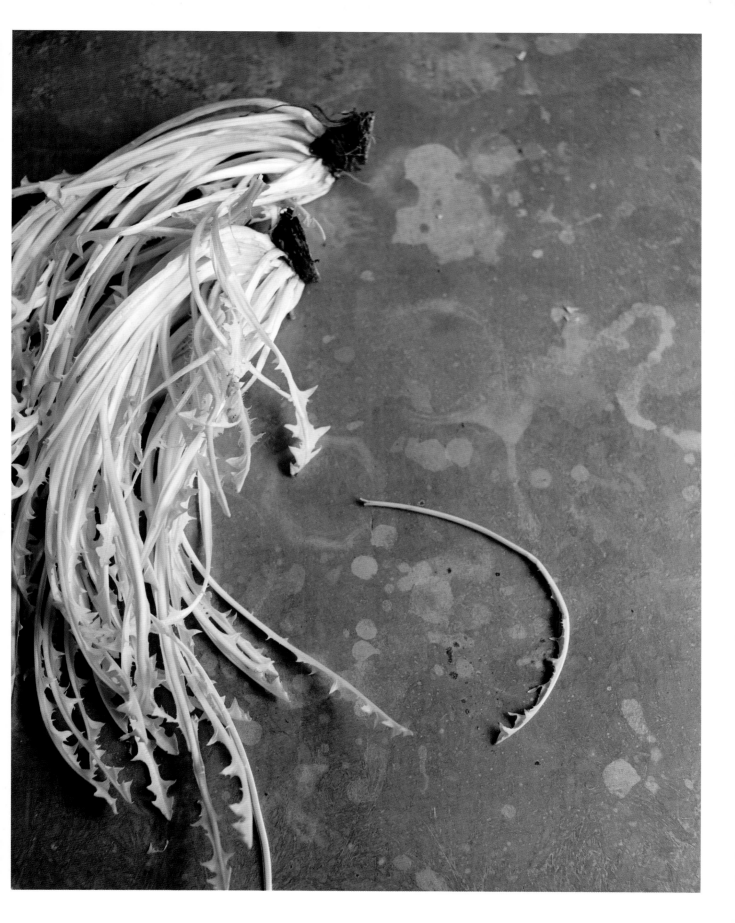

# ROOT
# VEGETABLES
*pages 92–133*

CONTENTS    **9**

HERBS, SPICES
AND NUTS
*pages 224–257*

# INTRODUCTION

I have written twenty-four books on the subject of Italian food, and one was specifically about Italian vegetables. You may wonder why I am tackling the subject again, but there are always fresh discoveries to be made in the world of food.

I learned about vegetables very early in my life. My parents did not have much money, and we were many children, so foraging in the countryside for vegetables 'for free' was very much part of our weekly, probably daily, pattern. I soon learned, possibly before I was six years old, to identify wild rocket, dandelion, asparagus, mustard, rape . . . and my ability to contribute to the family's food ingredients made me very proud indeed. The significance of that early foraging – which led to a lifelong passion for wild food in general – was brought back to me recently. In late 2015, I was in Australia making a TV series about the cultural aspects of Aboriginal food. Working with Richard Walley, the Elder of the Noongar tribe, I experienced pangs of nostalgia as I watched him and others gather and prepare food from the wild, food upon which their very lives depended. A nomadic people, they took only what they needed from nature then and there, ensuring that there would be food again when they returned to the same place – rather as I cut wild mushrooms, very carefully so that new growth is guaranteed the following season.

During the centuries, Italy has developed from a country that produced food for survival to a country whose food represents pleasure to many throughout the world. Its vegetable dishes are renowned, and indeed

Italian botanists have been responsible for the actual development of many of our best-known vegetables: think of calabrese (the broccoli from Calabria), edible peas and pods, cavolo nero, celery, fennel and globe artichokes. As these new ingredients were developed, so chefs and cooks were presented with the challenge of how best to cook them. Vegetable cooking in Italy is basically simple, relying on the flavour of each individual item to sing through, and the influences are varied, reflecting the cultures of those peoples who have lived in, conquered and influenced Italy throughout the centuries – the Romans and Greeks, the Arabs, the French.

Vegetables are very important in Italian food culture, and often, as in countries further to the east, will be at the heart of a dish, rather than an expensive protein such as meat. Many of the vegetables that we eat today have undergone an adventurous destiny, coming from the other side of the world, discovered by enterprising explorers. They encompass the fruits, seeds, roots, flower buds, leaves and stalks of plants, all of them with individual flavours, textures, colours, cooking qualities, and health benefits. Centuries ago, in 1611, an Italian called Giacomo Castelvetro lived in England and wrote a book, *The Fruit, Herbs and Vegetables of Italy*. He wanted to persuade the British to eat more fruit and vegetables. I like to think that I am doing much the same, introducing people to the joys of vegetables and the numerous ways of exploiting their delicacy and deliciousness. I hope I have succeeded. *Buon appetito*!

GREENS

I have had to divide this chapter into many sections and sub-sections because of the sheer complexity and divergences of the vegetables that we can call 'greens'. Mother Nature supplies such an enormous multitude of greens, and the Italians make great use of almost all of them (well, many of them were actually *bred* by the Italians!). Perhaps the largest class is the one with leaves, which are so numerous themselves that I have divided them into two sections: those such as spinach, which are usually cooked, and those such as lettuce or watercress, which are usually used raw in salads. Greens also include what I have called 'pods and seeds' such as beans and peas, and 'stalks and shoots' such as asparagus and globe artichokes. Finally, there is the huge family of brassicas, which includes cabbages and Brussels sprouts, cauliflower and broccoli… All these fall within the category of 'greens', and all are delicious cooked the Italian way.

## VEGETABLE LEAVES

Many of the vegetable leaves here are very Italian, but some of them are now becoming more widely available elsewhere. If you were truly interested, you could probably grow many of these leaves yourself, depending on climate – there are many Italian seed companies that can be found online.

*Barba di frate* (friar's beard), a vegetable that is also known in Italy as *agretti*, grows in bunches of long thin leaves that look like fat chives; the leaves taste nutty and salty rather than oniony. The vegetable is known in English as saltwort; it looks like a succulent seaweed, and grows mostly near the sea. In Latin its name is *Salsola soda*, and the vegetable was once burned, along with other seaweeds, to make soda ash or sodium carbonate (for soap and glass). I have never seen it for sale other than in Italy, although apparently it grows wild throughout Europe, and you can actually buy seeds (from an Italian company, of course) to grow at home. The washed leaves are briefly boiled or steamed and eaten like asparagus or samphire, dressed with oil and lemon. The vegetable is often sautéed, or cooked with tomatoes or with butter and breadcrumbs. *Barba di frate* is not all that popular yet abroad, but when in season – in late spring – it is very much in demand in Italy.

Chicories, with their slightly bitter flavour, are much loved in Italy, especially in the south. They come in a multitude of varieties. Perhaps the most familiar outside Italy is what the British know as **chicory**, spear-shaped heads of tight, pale green leaves, which are actually the blanched shoots of chicory roots after the above-ground leaves have grown and faded. It was developed in the early nineteenth century by a Belgian gardener, which is why it is familiarly known as Belgian chicory or endive, and c*icoria belga*; it is also known as *witloof* (white leaf). It is not an Italian vegetable, but we like it a lot in Italy: I eat it raw as salad and braise it with garlic, capers and tomatoes to eat as a side vegetable or accompanied by a double-crusted polenta cake (see page 46).

Most chicories, however, are loose heads of curly leaves which are known variously as endive, frisée, batavia, escarole and *catalogna*. **Curly endive** or **frisée** (*Indivia riccia*) comes in a tightish head of long and thin, dark green and raggedy leaves, looking rather like its ancestor, dandelion. **Escarole** or **batavia** is a looser head of leaves, but these are broader than curly endive, flat rather than curly, and paler in the middle. We love escarole in Italy, and it is grown everywhere, its outer leaves cooked as a vegetable, the inner leaves often used in salads. Curly endive is eaten in the same way.

*Catalogna* is another chicory only to be found in Italy as yet; it grows in bushy bunches of long leaves that look like dandelion. In Italian markets it may simply be labelled '*cicoria*'. There is also a *catalogna* that offers a new dimension, a vegetable developed from the original head of leaves, and this is one which contains *puntarelle* ('little shoots'). The bunches look similar to other chicories, but within the outer layer of leaves are small, pale green spears/shoots. These are delightfully tender when cooked, and look like large asparagus tips. Most *puntarelle* is reduced to julienne (often using a special cutter), and soaked in water to make the strips curl (and minimize bitterness) before eating or cooking. It is eaten as a salad dressed with anchovies, garlic oil and vinegar (see page 33). You will hear much more in the future about this vegetable. *Cicorietta* and dandelion are relations, but are used more in making salads (see page 86).

The *radicchio* family plays a large role in the world of Italian leaves. These wonderful dark red heads come in three principal varieties. ***Chioggia radicchio***, a round ball-like vegetable, is so called because it originated from the town of Chioggia (south of Venice). The colourful red and white leaves are mostly used for salads, to wrap food or to make sauces. ***Treviso radicchio***, a speciality of the town of Treviso (north of Venice), is also called *spadone* ('big sword') because of its elongated shape. It is available in the winter and has long sweetish leaves. It is excellent for salads but also for grilling and for preparing sauces for pasta and risottos. ***Castelfranco radicchio*** is a round head of yellowish leaves sprinkled with red, which are very beautiful, and are excellent for salads as they are mild in flavour. See also the section on Salad Leaves.

The leaves of Italian **spinach** (*spinacio*) are substantial and very wrinkled, and so require to be washed several times under cold running water. Spinach is very versatile: it can be used in many dishes from soups to fritters, from side dishes to purées, from fillings for pasta (*ravioli*, *cannelloni*, etc.) to fillings for pies and tarts, and small leaves can be eaten raw in salads. Spinach is one of the most used greens in Italy, especially in Tuscany, where dishes including spinach are mostly called '*a la fiorentina*'. (This, so they say, is because Catherine de' Medici – who left Florence to marry the King of France – loved spinach....)

The cultivated **Swiss chard** (*coste*) can grow quite big, looking rather like a giant cos lettuce on legs. The name 'chard' is derived from the French and Latin words for thistle; although chard is not a member of the thistle family, cardoon (see page 26) is, and it may be because cooked chard stalks have a similar texture to cardoon. The subspecies name '*cicla*' – the plant is classified botanically as *Beta vulgaris* var. *cicla* – comes from the Latin word *sicula*, meaning 'of Sicily', which is where the plant is thought to have originated.

It has two edible parts, the actual leaf and the large white stalk, which are cooked in different ways. The green is used like spinach or any other leaf vegetable, and the harder white part of the stem can be cooked as soup, braised as a vegetable, grilled or even fried in breadcrumbs. There is a wild variety called ***erbette***, which grows in the Ligurian hills, the leaves of which are mostly used as filling for the local ravioli, *pansôti*, in a mixture called *preboggion*.

See also the sections on Salad Leaves and Stalks and Shoots.

## BRASSICAS

The botanical family of brassicas includes a variety of vegetable foods which are extremely popular throughout all the Italian regions. Brassicas are mostly cooked in winter, and they produce very tasty peasant dishes. These have recently started to become popular in stylish restaurants, but they are first strongly 'revisited' to make them more appealing to the eye and taste, and more sophisticated.

The original brassica, **cabbage** (*cavolo*), is one of the oldest vegetables, having been eaten for thousands of years. The wild *Brassica oleracea* plant did not have a heart or head; leggy and loose-leafed, it would have looked and tasted rather like kale.

One cultivar of *B. oleracea* formed a head of loose or tight leaves, which gave us the blue-green, crinkly-leaved Savoy cabbage (*cavolo verza*) and the familiar tight-headed white cabbage (*cavolo cappuccio*). Savoy cabbages have loose curly leaves, which are particularly pretty on the outside: these are mostly used blanched as containers for various fillings, with the paler inside leaves used as other cabbages. I remember as a teenager, when food was relatively scarce, making an occasional salad from cabbage 'borrowed' from a nearby field. My friend and I would eat this, dressed with oil and vinegar, with bread for tea in the afternoon. Because of our persistent hunger, the taste was heaven indeed. But the best way of eating Savoy cabbage is in a soupy mess made with stale bread, Fontina, Parmesan, butter and stock (see page 45).

White cabbages, which consist of a head of much tighter leaves, can grow very large indeed and are eaten in various ways, notably in the fermented *Sauerkraut* or *Krauti*, which the Germans, Austrians and northern Italians like so much. Extremely finely cut white cabbage is fermented under weights in wooden barrels to extract moisture, after which it is cooked for some time before being served as a meat accompaniment. It plays a major part in a French dish called *choucroûte garnie*, fermented cabbage garnished with all sorts of pork meats; when the French reclaimed Alsace, they annexed the dish from Germany as well! The German original is called *Schlachterplatte*, a dish served when the slaughter of the pig takes place in winter. In Italy, with the exception of the north-east, white cabbage is eaten as a vegetable and in soups.

Red cabbage (*cavolo rosso*) is a tight-headed cabbage persuaded to change colour from green to red (some say as early as the sixteenth century). I like it very much for its design and pattern when you cut it in half. I don't care for it raw in salads (as many people do), but it is delightful cooked with a little vinegar and sugar, especially served with roast pork or, even better, roast goose. I usually add some raisins, which, when cooked, are sweet and juicy.

To the palette of cabbage colours has been added the so-called black cabbage or *cavolo nero*. Developed in Italy in the 1960s, its very dark green crinkled leaves on long stems have become very fashionable. It is most popular in Tuscany, where it plays a major part in *ribollita*, a bread and cabbage soup, best eaten the day after being cooked. In London the first to produce it was my late friend Alvaro Maccioni, owner of La Famiglia, a typical Tuscan restaurant. In fact, bread and cabbage are used in many different ways for their unity of taste.

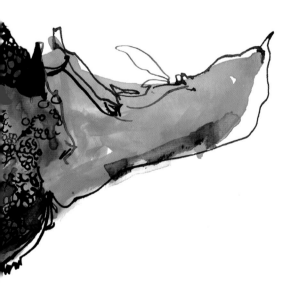

Other cabbage types retained heads of loose leaves, which can be quite bitter in flavour. These include the 'kale' of Scotland, the 'cole' of England, and the 'collards' of the American South. Another, if plucked early in spring, is what is known as spring greens. Spring greens and young kale can be very tender, and are eaten braised or boiled as a vegetable or soup. The wild sea kale, which I discuss briefly on page 27, is actually a maritime member of the cabbage family.

**Brussels sprouts** (*cavolini di Bruxelles*) – which look like miniature cabbages – are also a member of the cabbage family. They and their leaves are edible, and although they are not used so much in Italy, they deserve a mention. A near relation is flower sprouts (or kalettes), a cross between Brussels sprouts and kale, looking like miniature green and purple ruffled sprouts, an invention of the twenty-first century.

The origins of the brassicas **cauliflower** and **broccoli** are obscure, but cauliflower was known in Italy at the end of the fifteenth century (brought by the Moors, probably, from the Middle East), while broccoli hybrids have been developed only in the last couple of centuries. Cauliflower is a form of cabbage encouraged to flower, but in which the flowers have not developed beyond the bud stage. Clustered close together in a tight head, the white 'curd' is enclosed in edible cabbage-like leaves. **Cauliflower** (*cavolfiore*) is a very versatile vegetable. By boiling it in small florets until extremely tender, then mixing it with eggs and flour in a batter, you can produce delicious fritters. It makes a good purée too. Pasta and cauliflower were a staple combination in my family: my mother used to cook them together in a saucy concoction. Cauliflower is also delicious raw in salads or as a crudité, breadcrumbed and fried in *fritto misto*, and excellent pickled in an *insalata di rinforzo*.

*Broccolo romanesco* is a hybrid cauliflower, despite its name: its small, lively, green-coloured head is knobbly and conical, with florets in the shape of small pyramids. The beautiful colour is retained after cooking. This vegetable is used not only for soups and creams, but in salads, sautéed and boiled with lemon and oil. Cape broccoli is not a broccoli at all, but a pigmented cauliflower with a dark purple curd; this turns green when cooked.

And now we come to **broccoli**, the brassica that I think is the most popular and delicate of all. Broccoli is thought to be have been developed from its white cousin, cauliflower. Both are composed of stalk and 'cabbage' flower heads that remain in bud, clustered tightly together. Broccoli comes in several disparate forms, mostly developed in Italy. Sprouting broccoli was probably the first, as it has long stalks and separate smaller heads (the word '*broccoli*' means 'little arms' or 'little shoots' in Italian); these heads can be green, purple or white. Purple sprouting broccoli loses its colour when cooked, but it is delicious sautéed with garlic, chilli and oil and eaten as a vegetable or side dish. Calabrese is a later form, with a large, compact, blue-green head (its name meaning 'from Calabria'). It is used particularly in the south in a sauce for pasta, it also appears in soups, and can be a side dish vegetable at any time. *Broccolini* or Tenderstem broccoli ('Tenderstem' is now a trademark) is a cross between broccoli and *kai-lan*, also known as Chinese broccoli or kale.

**Cime di rapa** – literally 'tops of turnip' – are also known throughout Italy as *rapi* or *rapini*, and as *friarielli* or *broccoli di rapa* in Naples, and as *broccoletti* in Rome. Despite looking a bit like broccoli, and its many broccoli-related names, it is not really a broccoli at all, but a kind of rape (oilseed rape, *Brassica napus*), which is very closely related to turnip. (Turnip, although mostly classified as a root vegetable, is actually a brassica, its botanical name is *Brassica rapa rapa*.) Used in much the same way as sprouting broccoli, *cime di rapa* is very popular in the south of Italy.

**Kohlrabi**, known as 'turnip cabbage' (*cavolo rapa*), is probably the oddest-looking of all the brassicas. It resembles a sputnik, a round turnip-like vegetable (it's actually a root stem) studded with leaf stalks, either green (in summer) or purple (autumn and winter). The vegetable, after peeling, is cooked or eaten raw; the leaves can be cooked as well, just like kale.

Then there are shoots of a brassica, very much my favourite, which appear in cultivated fields in spring. They are from the mustard plant. What I pick are the still closed flowers before they open to become that wonderful yellow you see all over the countryside. They seed themselves later in the year and grow on the border of the mustard fields as an escape, allowing you to pick them without trespassing. They are delightful and you must pick them before they are sprayed. I eat them braised with crusty polenta . . . mmm! You can also eat the leaves earlier in the year, when they are known as mustard greens.

See also Roots (page 94).

# PODS AND SEEDS

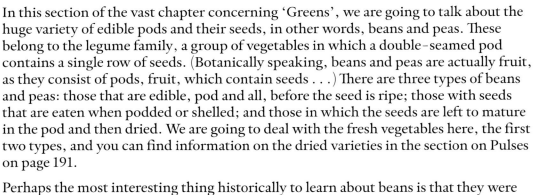

In this section of the vast chapter concerning 'Greens', we are going to talk about the huge variety of edible pods and their seeds, in other words, beans and peas. These belong to the legume family, a group of vegetables in which a double-seamed pod contains a single row of seeds. (Botanically speaking, beans and peas are actually fruit, as they consist of pods, fruit, which contain seeds . . .) There are three types of beans and peas: those that are edible, pod and all, before the seed is ripe; those with seeds that are eaten when podded or shelled; and those in which the seeds are left to mature in the pod and then dried. We are going to deal with the fresh vegetables here, the first two types, and you can find information on the dried varieties in the section on Pulses on page 191.

Perhaps the most interesting thing historically to learn about beans is that they were brought back from the Americas in what is known as the Columbian Exchange. Before Columbus discovered the New World, the only bean variety known in Europe was the fava or broad bean. These new plants – in their great variety, including haricot, black-eyed, cannellini, borlotti, butter and black beans – were embraced enthusiastically by everyone, as they were easy to grow, good to eat and could also be dried, which meant they could be enjoyed all year round. Beans have always been a good food for the impoverished, but now, of course, with the rediscovery of peasant food, they have become more sophisticated, and appear on the menus of chic restaurants...

First I would like to talk about the beans which are grown and appreciated for their fresh pods, generally known as 'green' – although this is a bit of misnomer, as a number of these vegetables, especially those most prized in Italy, come in many different colours. These mostly green beans (*fagiolini verdi*) include **haricots verts** or **French beans** (**string** or **snap beans** in the USA), whose pods are round, and **runner beans** (*fagiolini taccole* or *romano*), whose pods are flat. I presume the name for runner beans comes from the fact that they grow very quickly. They are mainly eaten when the tender pod is young, as it becomes too dry and woody to eat later on in the season. However, it is at this stage, when you leave the pod on the plant, that a wonderful multicoloured large bean is produced that can be cooked like any other large bean, after podding, or dried to cook later.

A particularly long variety of green bean, which measures about 30cm (12 inches) in length, is the originally Asian **yard-long** (or **asparagus**) **bean**. We grow a lot of this in the south of Italy. (I like that on Italian seed packets it is called *Fagiolo rampicante* – running rampant perhaps?!) Another bean we appreciate is the **wax bean**, which is virtually the same in look and taste as the green bean, but its pod is cream-coloured, while its tiny beans are lime green.

Green beans should be eaten when young, when the pods are very tender. At one point, the sides of these beans had to be de-stringed (it's why they have the name 'string'), but now most green beans have been bred to be stringless. Often these bright green beans can turn out a muddy olive green when boiled. This is caused by the chlorophyll in the beans reacting with acids in the cooking water. You should cook the beans in plenty of water, so that the acids are diluted, and never cover with a lid, thereby allowing the acids to escape. My preferred way of cooking all these beans, though, is to stew them in a tomato, garlic and basil sauce, accompanied by bread for a starter.

And now we come to the beans which are podded, and the 'seeds' eaten. Prime among them in Italy, particularly in the north, is the **borlotti bean**, which can be found fresh in late summer. The beans are beige streaked with magenta, and turn brown when cooked: the pods are magenta and white, easily the most colourful of all the beans. Many times as a child I was 'commanded' to pod the borlotti beans for *minestrone* or *pasta e fagioli or fagioli in insalata* with onion and tuna.

**Cannellini beans** are the next most popular in Italy, especially in Tuscany, but these are most commonly eaten dried (see page 191).

The **broad bean**, the only one of the huge bean family to be native to the West, is another podded bean used fresh. (However, if you grow them yourself, you can eat the pods too if you catch them young enough, see page 70.) In Italy, the podded beans are generally eaten raw and very young, in Puglia accompanied by fresh Pecorino cheese, bread and a good glass of wine. If the beans are a little older, you can cook them briefly and remove the sludge-green outer skin, revealing the inner brilliant green seed. Fresh, you will find broad beans cooked together with peas, onions and artichokes in the Sicilian *frittedda*, a lovely stew of the springtime vegetable. Broad beans are known as fava and Windsor beans in the USA; the American lima beans, known also as butter beans, are closely related to broad beans, and are eaten in the same way.

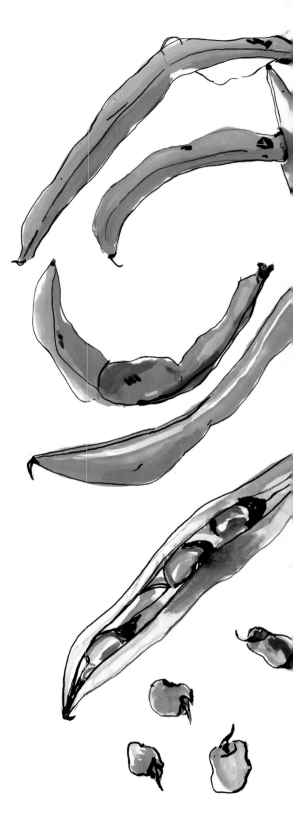

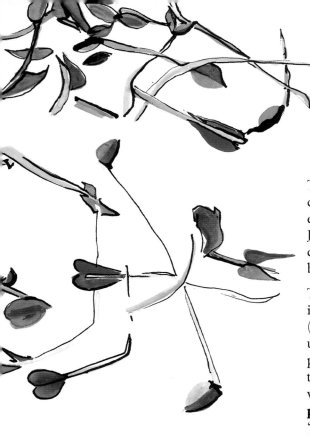

The **edamame bean** (*fagiolo soia*) is an immature soya bean cooked in the pod. The beans are sprinkled with sea salt, and you eat them by sucking the beans out of the pod. Very popular in Japanese restaurants, these beans have a wonderful pale green colour and taste very nutty. You could combine the podded beans with onion and tuna for a salad.

The **pea** is an ancient vegetable. When dried, it used to be an important form of protein in ancient times. **Garden peas** (*piselli*), varieties that can be eaten fresh, were not developed until the sixteenth century in Italy. The inner skins of garden pea pods were inedible, so the peas were always removed from the pods. It wasn't until at least a century later that a pea pod was cultivated without that inedible inner skin. The **mangetout pea**, or *taccole* in Italy, is edible, pod and all (thus the French 'eat-all' and the Italian *mangiatutto*), and is eaten when the pod is still flat, before the peas begin to swell. **Snow peas** are similar, but the peas are in a later stage of growth. The American **sugar-snap peas** have even larger peas within the pods, but are still edible, pod and all, and much sweeter than any of the other peas (apart from *petits pois*). All these pea varieties are best stewed with tomatoes, or just boiled with butter.

The pea is found in almost all cuisines of the world, eaten both fresh and dried. From my garden I used to eat them raw because of their sweetness. In supermarkets and greengrocers they are often not very tender – because they have been hanging about for a while – and sometimes I use frozen peas instead, as I can be sure they are truly sweet – they are frozen straight from the field, when very young and tender (as are most broad and soya beans). Frozen ***petits pois*** are garden peas picked at a very early stage of development, and are very sweet indeed. *Risi e bisi*, the famous risotto of Venice, is an amalgam of rice and peas. *Frittata di piselli*, *pasta e piselli*, *piselli al prosciutto*, *zuppa di piselli* and *piselli e patate* are among the many Italian ways to use peas.

Recently developed and in fashion are **pea shoots**, which are the tips of the pea plant; these are used as a green vegetable or for decoration of 'modern' dishes.

# STALKS AND SHOOTS

Stalk, stem and shoot vegetables are growths from plant roots, namely the parts of the plant that grow above ground. They are quite rare among edible plants, as they do not on the whole form fruits or leaves: it is the stalks, stems or shoots themselves that are eaten.

Primary in this group are asparagus, cardoon, celery and my own particular favourite, hop shoots. Growing similarly, and many of them considered here, are Swiss chard, fennel, sea kale and, perhaps surprisingly, rhubarb. Globe artichokes are also included in this section because it is the stalk or stem buds, the immature flower heads, that are eaten. Kohlrabi, although it is a swollen stem, is discussed in the Brassica section (see page 21).

**Asparagus** (*asparago*) is the best example of a shoot vegetable. It is a member of the lily family, as are garlic, leek and onion. There are several varieties available: green, white, purple – which come in different thicknesses – and wild asparagus. The latter grows in the wild throughout Europe. I will never forget travelling by car through Sardinia: at various points along the roadside shepherds were selling bundles of wild asparagus, which they had collected while grazing their sheep. (This often happens in Italy, with many different items, grown in the wild or in a garden plot, offered for sale: fresh wild mushrooms or whatever is locally in season. It's a joy to take home such fresh produce, for certain organically grown.)

Asparagus stems or spears grow from an underground rhizome, known as a crown. Spears can be male or female. Female spears are less productive because they put much of their energy into producing red berries, which are mildly poisonous to humans. (Asparagus is the only vegetable in the lily family to bear seeds and not fruit.) Male hybrids are the ones most available commercially, because they concentrate on spear production! The spears are cut from the ground when the tips are still firm and closed; if allowed to grow on, frondy growth would develop from the tips.

Green and white asparagus, although they look so different, are the same plant. The white is deliberately blanched by growing it totally under the earth (or, often today, polythene). It is never exposed to sunlight, in order to prevent the development of green chlorophyll. This type of asparagus is tender and subtle in flavour, and the Germans, French and Spanish are particularly fond of it. It is eaten in Germany freshly boiled with new potatoes, melted butter and big slices of Black Forest ham. The French prefer it with sauce hollandaise. The only part of Italy where white asparagus is grown is in the Veneto, in the area of Bassano del Grappa, where the local restaurants hold competitions to see who produces the best white asparagus dish.

Green asparagus, which is preferred in Britain, America and Australia, is allowed to grow naturally out of the earth, bathed in sunlight, in order to encourage the green coloration, and it is collected when still very tender. There are a myriad ways of cooking asparagus: obviously you can plainly steam or boil it and serve it with melted butter or hollandaise; but you could add a little freshly grated Parmesan as well. You could roast thicker spears of asparagus, cook them with onions and eggs, purée them as a *ravioli* filling, and serve them whole baked in a quiche or tart.

Purple asparagus was developed from green, and is so tender from tip to base that it can be eaten raw; wonderful for dipping and salads. Italian growers were responsible, and they gave it the name 'Violetto d'Albenga'. 'Burgundine' is a purple asparagus now being grown in Britain.

Another shoot, which looks like mini asparagus, is the **hop shoot**. The hop is the plant that produces flower heads/cones that are used to flavour beer. When the plants are under cultivation, they are cut right back at the end of the season; numerous new shoots then grow from the rootstock in spring. It is these that can be cut (so long as you leave one or two to grow on for beer production!), and cooked, often being called 'the poor man's asparagus'. In Italy hop shoots can be collected from the hedges (as they probably can in hop-growing areas of England), and used in *frittatas*, risottos and salads. In springtime you can find hop shoots in the markets of Venice, labelled as *bruscandoli*. They are sold in small bunches by farmers, who have collected the shoots on the many islands of the lagoon. In Belgium, a famous beer-producing country like England, hop shoots are a local speciality: they are often blanched to produce white rather than green shoots. You could grow hops yourself at home: buy plants and site them where they can climb up a hedge or a wall.

The **cardoon** (*cardo*) is a member of the edible thistle family, as is the globe artichoke. In fact it is thought that the wild cardoon – native to the Mediterranean and North Africa – may be the ancestor of both vegetables. Left to grow, cardoon plants can reach a height of 1.8 metres (6 feet), with a typical purple thistle flower. However, it is the cardoon ribs and stalks that are eaten, not the flower buds or heads. The plant looks like celery, with flatter, longer and wider silver stalks growing in clumps, surrounded by silvery-green leaves. They need to be extensively trimmed before being used – you have to get rid of all but the very white bottom stalks, and there are many prickly outer leaves and strings.

The cardoon is very much loved in various parts of Italy. In Piedmont they blanch the stalks by bending them over and banking them up with earth. This keeps the stalks white and tender, and they are known colloquially as *gobbi*, 'hunchbacks'. Young fresh stalks are mainly used raw in Piedmont to be dipped into *bagna cauda* (the anchovy and garlic dip) at Christmas time. More mature stalks are used in soups, in flans, in *frittatas* and baked: I love pieces of cardoon breadcrumbed and deep-fried.

But perhaps the most intriguing stalk or stem vegetable is the **globe artichoke** (*carciofo*), which, like cardoons, belongs to the thistle family. It is the tender parts of the unopened flower buds – and residual stalk – that are eaten, rather than the ribs and stalks, as with the cardoon. If allowed to grow on, like cardoon, the plant would reach a good height, and the head would develop into a classic thistle flower. It was the Italians who brought it into successful cultivation, and it is still in Italy that it remains most popular, being such a staple food in season that in the south they sell them in big bundles for virtually nothing! Artichokes are predominant in Rome and Lazio, part of the Jewish food culture. There are many varieties available, and many sizes: in Italy, the biggest, *la mamma*, is the one to appear at the top of the stalk; secondary heads, which grow later below the main head, are called *figli* (children); and the smallest heads, which grow last and furthest down the stalk, are called *nipoti* (nephews).

What you eat of the artichoke are the tender fleshy parts at the base of the leaves (the rest of the leaves are simply too tough), and the heart, bottom or 'fond'. You must first remove the prickly central choke (of a mature vegetable), which is what would develop into a flower. Most artichokes are boiled whole to eat as a starter with melted butter, vinaigrette or a sauce like hollandaise. They can be stuffed and braised or even preserved in vinegar and kept in olive oil for *antipasti*. If they are very young and small, artichokes can be eaten raw, very thinly sliced. In Italy and many places on the Continent, globe artichokes are sold ready prepared, the hearts only, and these can be cooked together with onion, olives and potatoes, fried in a batter, roasted on a grill, fried in oil. An essence of artichokes is used in an aperitif called Cynar, which also serves as a digestif.

The stalk **celery** (*sedano*) and its close relative celeriac (see page 98) were both developed by the Italians in the seventeenth

century from a wild plant, called smallage. There are several closely related types: white celery has been blanched in cultivation (by earthing up or covering with polythene); green celery, which is stronger in flavour, is unblanched; and a Chinese celery (*kun choi*), which is occasionally available, is like very small celery with hollow thin stalks. Celery is eaten raw (*pinzimonio*) – good for dips and with cheese (in the English fashion). As a foundation vegetable, it is cooked in a '*soffritto*' in Italy, with onion and other root vegetables as the start of a *ragù* sauce, for instance. Elsewhere it is often used in the same fashion, as the basis of a stock, stew or soup. Celery leaves and seeds can also be used, as they carry a good celery flavour.

There are three basic types of **fennel** (*finocchio*), also classified as a stem or stalk vegetable. A wild form still grows wild in Italy, and is now used mainly for its seed as a spice. Sweet fennel is closely related, and it is grown for its feathery leaves (herb) and seeds (spice). The Italians developed a third type around the late seventeenth century; known as Florence or bulb fennel, this is used as a vegetable. The base of the stem or stalk was encouraged to expand and swell, forming a bulb with overlapping layers of 'leaves'. These bulbs can be squat and rounded, or elongated (female and male); the females have the best flavour. Bulb fennel is blanched during cultivation (earthed up or covered with polythene) to keep it white and to sweeten its gloriously aniseedy flesh. I love fennel raw (*pinzimonio*) with dips like *bagna cauda* (see page 166), and sliced thinly in salads. Raw, it is often served after a meal in Italy, as it is considered a digestive. It is good cooked (although much of the anise flavour is lost), and served with light meat and fish. I have developed a way of using fennel as a sauce for pasta, which is delicious with prawns (see page 83).

**Sea kale** (*cavolo marino*) is another shoot and stalk vegetable, which grows wild on beaches in Europe. In cultivation it is blanched, so that it has fat, succulent white stalks, which can be eaten like asparagus. It is rarely found in markets, so I have not given a recipe. Yet another stalk is that of **rhubarb** (*rabarbaro*), which, although botanically a vegetable, is eaten as a fruit, so has no natural place here. And a final stalk vegetable is **Swiss chard**; both stalks and leaves are eaten, and I talk about them elsewhere (see page 18). **Celtuce**, known as *wosun* in China, is a cultivar of lettuce, grown for its thick stem: this is shaved thinly and eaten raw or cooked, or chopped and sliced and stir-fried.

# SALAD LEAVES

By 'salad leaves', I mean those leaves – green, red, yellow, a myriad colours – that are mostly eaten raw in salads (although some of them can be cooked). To this group also belong 'wild' leaves, most of which are easy to collect and find, provided you have access to the countryside. As a child in the spring, I would go either with my parents or some neighbouring farmer through the fields in search of small and tender dandelions, nettles, wild garlic and, a little later in the year, wild rocket and sorrel. All these items are essential, whether wild or cultivated, for a good salad, and the more the merrier. The French call a salad of mixed leaves '*mesclun*' (meaning, appropriately, 'big mixture'), and on the Continent you can find such combinations for sale on market stalls.

I shall start, though, with **lettuce** in all its variety. The botanical name of lettuce is *Lactuca sativa* (*lattuga* in Italian). '*Lac*' means milk in Latin, which is an allusion to the white substance, now called latex, exuded by cut stems. This latex is mildly narcotic, which is possibly why Beatrix Potter's famous Flopsy Bunnies fell asleep after gorging on Mr McGregor's lettuces – and why health writers say that lettuce is a good thing to eat at night.

Three types of lettuce are most worthy of note. The most common in the UK, known as **round lettuce**, has floppy, loosely bunched leaves and is the most widely planted, used mainly in salads. The lettuces known as **Romaine** and **Cos** – they are the same (*lattuga romana*) – have loose heads of long leaves, which are much crisper than round lettuces. These are used mainly for salads, sandwiches and for dipping and stuffing, and have a starring role in Caesar salads. (The name 'Romaine' came from the Romans, who grew them, while Cos are thought to be have been developed on the Greek island of Cos.) Little gem lettuces are a compact variety of Cos/Romaine lettuce. The third type of lettuce is the crisphead, better known as **iceberg** (*lattuga iceberg!*), which is used in salads and as containers for salad ingredients.

The Italians, once again, have developed many different types of leaves to be used in salads, including the loose-leaved *lollo rosso* (crinkled leaves tinged deep red at their ends), *lollo biondo* and *lollo verde*. Oakleaf lettuces, loose-leaved again, have serrated green leaves, sometimes tinged with red. But we must not forget other cultivated leaves that can happily be used in salads: the chicories such as curly endive or frisée, escarole or batavia, and the various types of radicchio (all discussed in the section on Vegetable Leaves on page 16). Small chard leaves – green with red stalks and spines – can be plucked young and used in salads, as can other young leaves, particularly spinach. A Japanese leaf, a mustard green known as mizuna, forms part of many pre-packed salad mixes, and adds texture and good mustardy flavour.

**Watercress** (*crescione*) is a wonderful leaf to add to salads, with its peppery and pungent flavour. Unlike other salad leaves, it is grown in streams, in clean running water, and can be cultivated or collected from the wild. Most of us, unfortunately, have to buy it in closed plastic bags. However, it is still good, used raw in salads or as a garnish; it makes magnificent sauces and soups, and adds savour to sandwiches. The botanical name of watercress is *Nasturtium officinale*, which points in the direction of another salad ingredient that can be grown or collected: the actual garden flower **nasturtium** (*nasturzio*). Apparently the name means 'twisting the nose' in Latin, referring to its strong scent: the buds, flowers and leaves are incredibly peppery in flavour.

As a child I used to collect **corn salad**, **lamb's lettuce**, or **mâche** (*valeriana*) from the wild, but the cultivated variety, bought usually in packets, is very tender and is a delicious addition to any salad. Apparently it has the name 'corn' because it used to grow as a weed in grain fields: I used to collect it from between the rows of vines in the local vineyards. **Rocket** (*rucola* in Italian, which became *arugula* in the USA) is another salad leaf that has become popular, fashionable indeed, but it is one I could find growing wild in the northern Italian countryside. Its sharp taste – almost of horseradish, it is so peppery – adds immeasurably to a mixed green salad. It is very easy to grow at home, and is delicious dressed with a good oil and with shavings of Parmesan on top. Commercially, I feel rocket has been over-exposed, so it is not so interesting any more . . .

What is known as **mustard and cress** (again *crescione*) is actually a combination of two herbs, garden cress (*Lepidium sativum*) and white mustard (*Brassica hirta*). The seeds are scattered on damp kitchen paper, or cotton wool (or similar) and, after germination, the tiny plants are cut when they are some 5cm (2 inches) tall. The combination of the two, the mustard spicy, the cress blander, is delicious as a garnish, or in a sandwich in the British style. Sadly, some punnets sold in British supermarkets have been found to be composed of oilseed rape seeds with a small amount of cress, which is not nearly so tasty.

Now to the truly wild leaves. The **dandelion**, *Taraxacum officinalis*, is the weed plant known as '*piss-en-lit*' in French and '*piscialetto*' in Italian, so called because it has diuretic properties. You can find it for sale in Italian markets as simply *cicoria di campo*, as its bitter flavour is reminiscent of many of the chicories. If you choose young leaves, and clean them well, dandelion leaves make a wonderful salad leaf (look at my springtime salad on page 86), and can also be cooked, with beans and pork, say.

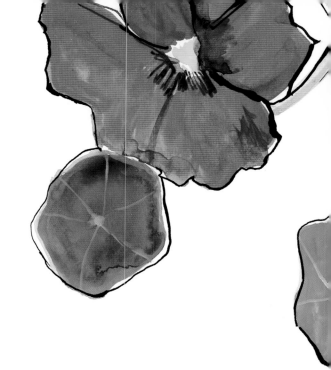

The tender leaves of **wild sorrel** (*acetosa*) are ideal for salad in that they give an amazing acidity. They are also good in risottos or soups. You can grow sorrel in your garden, one of the first plants to appear in the spring. As a child, I used to chew sorrel stems because of their pleasant sour taste. Another wild leaf, that of wild garlic, I talk about in the Garlic section on page 100.

And finally the **nettle** (*ortica*), the stinging leaf of a weed that grows everywhere throughout Europe (usually near human settlements, oddly enough). These leaves contain many more natural goodies than they do taste, but it's still worthwhile picking them to eat (please, always with gloves on!). Nettle leaves are actually cooked rather than eaten raw, for a filling for pies and *ravioli*, in risottos and in soups. My tongue still remembers the taste of the wild herb soup that Nina, my farmer/hotelier friend from the Aosta Valley, used to make: she would go into the local fields and collect at least ten different wild greens growing in that very short season at 1,800 metres (6,000 feet) above sea level. She would make with them what she called THE BEST SOUP IN THE WORLD!

## INSALATA DI PUNTARELLE
*Puntarelle Salad*

Puntarelle, a delightful vegetable, is a development of the chicory plant called catalogna, which is used quite a lot, particularly in Rome. The Italians like bitterness in their vegetables, and puntarelle, the little shoots grown from the centre of the vegetable, are delicate and extremely tender, to be cooked or eaten raw in salads.

Cut the puntarelle shoots from the head of catalogna, to about 7–8cm (3 inches) long. Cut them lengthways to the size of matchsticks. Put them into iced water, where they will curl and lose some bitterness.

Prepare the sauce. Mash the anchovies in a bowl, using a fork, then add the garlic, olive oil, vinegar, a little salt and plenty of pepper.

Drain the puntarelle well, dress with the sauce, and serve. Eat as a side salad or a starter.

SERVES 4

—1 head of catalogna with puntarelle (see page 17)

SAUCE
—6 anchovy fillets in oil, drained
—1 small garlic clove, peeled and crushed
—4 tablespoons extra virgin olive oil
—2 tablespoons white wine vinegar
—salt and freshly ground black pepper

*vegetable leaves*

# CALZONE DI SCAROLA
## *Batavia Folded Pizza*

Escarole or batavia – *scarola* in Italian – is a leafy plant of the chicory family, which is used fresh in salads and cooked as a filling. In the south of Italy they usually call this dish *pizza di scarola*, but I am putting the escarole filling individually in pastry in the shape of a *calzone*, which is a folded pizza!

Preheat the oven to 180°C (350°F/gas 4).

Wash and dry the green leaves, and chop them coarsely.

In a frying pan, heat 4 tablespoons of olive oil. Add the garlic, stir, then immediately add the tomatoes, the chopped leaves, capers, raisins and some salt and pepper to taste. Put a lid on and braise the leaves until soft, about 15 minutes. Let the mixture cool, then squeeze out the majority of the liquid, using your hands.

On a lightly floured surface, roll out the pastry to a 5mm (¼ inch) thickness. Cut into four circles of equal diameter, roughly 25cm (10 inches). Place a quarter of the vegetable mixture in the middle of each circle. Pull one side of the circle over the filling, then fold over the edges to enclose, or very firmly fork the two layers together. You will have a half-moon *calzone*.

Place them on a baking sheet and brush with a little olive oil. Bake in the preheated oven for 20–30 minutes. Serve hot or cold.

SERVES 4

—500g (1lb 2oz) shortcrust pastry

FILLING
—600g (1lb 5oz) batavia or escarole (or dandelion or frisée)
—extra virgin olive oil
—2 garlic cloves, peeled and sliced
—2 medium tomatoes, finely chopped
—20g (¾oz) salted capers, desalted (see page 75)
—20g (¾oz) soft raisins
—salt and freshly ground black pepper

# PALLINE DI SPINACI
*Spinach Fritters*

This is one of the most successful fritters I have ever created, and it has been very popular in Carluccio's for many years, served as an additional decoration to a plate of pasta with a courgette (zucchini) sauce (and a donation goes to charity with every plate sold). The fritters also make ideal canapés or finger food.

Wash the spinach well, removing any tough stalks, then blanch in boiling slightly salted water for a few minutes. Drain well. When cool enough to handle, squeeze the excess water out and chop the leaves coarsely.

Place in a bowl and add the breadcrumbs, beaten eggs, a couple of grates of nutmeg, the garlic and the Parmesan. Season to taste with salt and pepper. Mix well. If the mixture appears too wet, add some more breadcrumbs.

Form the mixture into little round balls the size of walnuts, and shallow-fry in hot olive oil until softly brown, about 4–5 minutes on each side. Drain on absorbent kitchen paper, and serve warm or cold.

MAKES 24

—600g (1lb 5oz) fresh spinach
—80g (2³/₄oz/1¹/₂ cups) fresh white breadcrumbs
—2 medium eggs, beaten
—freshly grated nutmeg
—1 garlic clove, peeled and crushed
—50g (1³/₄oz) Parmesan, freshly grated
—salt and freshly ground black pepper
—olive oil, for shallow-frying

# INDIVIA 'MBUTTUNATA
## *Stuffed Curly Endive*

In Jewish cuisine in Rome, the endive was fried in olive oil without the stuffing on each side until crisp. I prefer it stuffed and then baked in the oven as southern Italian peasants do, calling it 'buttoned-up endive'.

Preheat the oven to 180°C (350°F/gas 4).

Trim the heads of the endives by tidying the outer leaves, removing any green tops that are less than crisp. Blanch the heads in boiling salted water for about 4–5 minutes, just to soften the leaves. Leave to cool.

For the stuffing, mix the breadcrumbs with all the other stuffing ingredients, seasoning well with salt and pepper.

When the endives are cool, spread the leaves open, revealing their centres. Fill this with the stuffing mixture, sprinkle with 2 tablespoons of the olive oil, and close by pulling the other leaves into the centre. Tie each endive into a round shape using two pieces of string.

Place on a baking tray and sprinkle with the remaining olive oil. Bake in the preheated oven for 25 minutes or so, until the point of a sharp knife goes in easily.

Serve warm, halved or quartered, or serve a half portion as a generous starter.

SERVES 4

—2 medium heads of curly endive, about 700g (1lb 9oz), well washed and dried
—3 tablespoons extra virgin olive oil

STUFFING
—100g (3½oz/2 cups) fresh white breadcrumbs
—30g (1oz) pine nuts
—20g (¾oz) soft raisins
—50g (1¾oz) Pecorino cheese, freshly grated
—2 medium garlic cloves, peeled and very finely puréed
—6 tablespoons extra virgin olive oil
20g (¾oz) small salted capers, desalted (see page 75)
—2 medium eggs, beaten
—salt and freshly ground black pepper

# RAVIOLI CON SPINACI
## *Ravioli with Spinach*

Filled pastas, like *ravioli*, *cannelloni* or *crespelle*, are wonderful vehicles for any sort of leftovers. A spinach and ricotta filling, although it is very simple, is delightful.

Make the pasta first. Sift the flour on to a work surface, and form into a mound with a well in the centre. Break the eggs into the well, and add the salt. Mix the eggs into the flour with your hands, until you have a coarse paste. Scrape up any sticky bits with a spatula, and add a little more flour if necessary. Clean the work surface before starting to knead. Knead the dough for 10–15 minutes – yes, sorry, it needs that time! – until the consistency is smooth and elastic. Wrap the dough in clingfilm (plastic wrap) and rest in a cool place for 30 minutes.

For the filling, blanch the spinach in boiling salted water for a few minutes, then drain. When cool enough to handle, squeeze the excess water out and chop coarsely. Mix with the ricotta, nutmeg, grated Parmesan, beaten egg, and salt and pepper to taste.

Unwrap the dough and roll it out on a lightly floured surface to thin sheets, 5mm (¼ inch) thick (a machine will do this easily for you!). Cut into bands 8cm (3 inches) wide. Place 1 teaspoon of the filling every 6–7cm (2½ inches) along the middle of one pasta band. Brush around each pile of mixture with water. Cover with another pasta band, and press all around each pile of mixture to get the air out and to make the pasta sheets adhere to each other. Using a serrated pastry or ravioli wheel, cut out each raviolo to about 7cm (2½ inches) square. Cover with a clean dry cloth and leave to rest for a while.

When ready to serve, boil the ravioli in salted water for 4–5 minutes. Drain well. Melt the butter in a pan and add the sage. Toss in the ravioli, sprinkle with Parmesan and serve.

—200g (7oz / about 1¼ cups) Italian '00' flour
—2 medium eggs
—a pinch of salt

**FILLING**
—250g (9oz) fresh spinach
—salt and freshly ground black pepper
—150g (5½oz / ¾ cup) fresh ricotta cheese
—½ teaspoon freshly grated nutmeg
—25g (1oz) Parmesan, freshly grated
—1 medium egg, beaten

**TO SERVE**
—75g (2¾oz) unsalted butter
—3–4 fresh sage leaves, finely chopped
—50g (1¾oz) Parmesan, freshly grated

*vegetable leaves*

SERVES 4

# TORTA PASQUALINA
*Swiss Chard and Artichoke Tart*
*Pages 42–3*

# TORTA PASQUALINA
## Swiss Chard and Artichoke Tart

It is an Easter tradition in Liguria to bake this tart, often to take on the compulsory picnic, pasquetta, on Easter Monday. It is based on erbette, a wild green variety of Swiss chard that grows on the surrounding hills. Artichokes are cultivated not far away and the delicate Ligurian olive oil is also local.

Heat 6 tablespoons of the olive oil in a large lidded pan. Add the artichoke hearts, onion, capers, parsley and a little water, and braise, covered, until tender, about 10–15 minutes. Drain.

Blanch the Swiss chard leaves in salted water for a few minutes, then drain. When cool enough to handle, squeeze out the water and chop the leaves coarsely.

Mix the Swiss chard with the ricotta and the beaten eggs, the Parmesan, a few grates of nutmeg and some salt and pepper to taste. Add the artichoke mixture and mix well together.

Preheat the oven to 200°C (400°F/gas 6). On a lightly floured surface, roll the pastry out to a 5mm (¼ inch) thickness. Grease a fluted 27cm (10½ inch) loose-bottomed tart tin with a little olive oil, then line with the pastry. Cut off any surplus, which you will need for the lattice. Line the pastry in the tin with baking paper and baking beans, then blind-bake for 10 minutes. Remove the beans, and cook for a further 5 minutes to crisp the base. Cut the remaining pastry into thin strips.

Pour the filling into the pastry-lined tart tin, push in the quail's eggs, and cover with a lattice of pastry strips. Brush these with the beaten egg, then bake in the preheated oven for 35 minutes. Serve hot or cold.

SERVES 6–8

—1kg (2lb 4oz) shortcrust pastry
—1 medium egg, beaten

FILLING
—extra virgin olive oil
—12 small raw artichoke hearts, halved (if cleaning the artichokes yourself, remove the tough outer leaves and scrape out the fluffy choke in the centre, if there is one)
—1 small onion, peeled and finely chopped
—1 tablespoon salted capers, desalted (see page 75)
—1 small bunch of fresh flat-leaf parsley, chopped
—1kg (2lb 4oz) Swiss chard leaves (not stalks), or spinach
—250g (9oz/1 cup) fresh ricotta cheese
—4 medium eggs, beaten
—60g (2¼oz) Parmesan, freshly grated
—freshly grated nutmeg
—12 quail's eggs, boiled for 3 minutes and shelled
—salt and freshly ground black pepper

# ZUPPA DI CAVOLO VALDOSTANA
*Cabbage Soup Aosta Valley Style*

If you are in the Aosta Valley in winter and visit a local restaurant or *osteria*, you may find this heart-warming and delicious soup or *pasticcio* on the menu. It is based on cabbage, and two wonderful products of the Aosta Valley, Fontina cheese and Alpine butter.

Put the cabbage into a pan with a little salt and the stock, and boil until soft and tender, about 15–20 minutes. Remove the cabbage from the liquid, and put to one side to cool. Reserve the liquid.

Preheat the oven to 200°C (400°F/gas 6).

Cut the bread into big cubes. Heat the olive oil and the butter together in a frying pan, and fry the bread cubes for a few minutes, until golden. Drain on absorbent kitchen paper.

In a large ovenproof dish, build layers of cabbage, bread cubes and Fontina cheese. Add some of the reserved cabbage cooking stock, which will penetrate to the bottom layer and soften the bread. Sprinkle this with some of the Parmesan, then layer again until the ingredients have all been used up. Finish with the remainder of the stock.

When ready to bake, fry the garlic in a small frying pan in the butter until foaming, then pour on top of the cabbage.

Bake in the preheated oven for 25–30 minutes. Before serving, mix the cabbage around with a spoon and serve, sprinkled with pepper.

SERVES 4

—800g (1lb 12oz) Savoy cabbage, cleaned and chopped
—1.5 litres (2¾ pints/6 cups) chicken or vegetable stock
—2 large thick slices of wholegrain bread
—4 tablespoons extra virgin olive oil
—40g (1½oz) Alpine butter
—300g (10½oz) Fontina cheese, shredded or sliced
—60g (2¼ oz) Parmesan, freshly grated
—salt and freshly ground black pepper

TO FINISH
—2 garlic cloves, peeled and sliced
—60g (2¼oz) unsalted butter

*brassicas*

**45**

# CIME DI RAPA E CICORIA BELGA CON CROSTA DI POLENTA
*Polenta Crust with Broccoli and Chicory*

The nearest most people will be able to get to the Italian favourite, *cime di rape* (actually a form of rape), are small spears of purple sprouting broccoli. In the south of Italy, when *cime di rape* is in season, it is constantly used, mostly as a side dish to fish and meat, but also by itself as a *minestra*, braised to be eaten with bread. The combination with chicory and polenta, as here, is my favourite.

To start cooking the vegetables, heat the olive oil in a large saucepan and lightly fry the garlic. Add the rape tops or broccoli, the chicory, capers and a little water, then cover with a lid and cook until tender, about 10–15 minutes. Add the chilli, and some salt and pepper to taste, and gently simmer for 2 minutes.

Meanwhile, to make the polenta crust – a sort of cake – place the polenta in a bowl and add about 250ml (9fl oz/1 cup) of hot water, with some salt and 3 tablespoons of the olive oil. Mix well. Flatten with your hand to a rough hamburger size, keeping it as one cake. Fry in a suitably sized frying pan, in the remaining oil, until first one side and then the other is darkish brown and forms a crust. This should take about 8 minutes on each side.

Eat the polenta cake cut into wedges, together with the vegetables.

SERVES 4–6

—5 tablespoons extra virgin olive oil
—1 garlic clove, peeled and finely sliced
—500g (1lb 2oz) *cime di rape*, just the broccoli-like tops (or small broccoli florets)
—450g (1lb) Belgian chicory, the chicons cut in half
—a few salted capers, desalted (see page 75) and chopped
—1 small chilli, finely sliced
—salt and freshly ground black pepper

POLENTA CRUST
—375g (13oz/2 cups) fine instant polenta (instant cornmeal)
—6 tablespoons extra virgin olive oil

# ORECCHIETTE CON BROCCOLI E COZZE
## *Broccoli and Mussel Pasta*

This is a very pleasant pasta dish from the south of Italy, which uses locally produced ingredients. One of these is the Pugliese hand-made pasta called *orecchiette*, 'little ears', which is known all over Puglia, but is very typical of the town of Bari.

Thoroughly clean the mussels. Wash them in cold water, using a stiff brush to scrape off any barnacles, and pull out the stringy 'beard', if there is one. If any mussels gape open, discard them.

Cook the pasta in boiling salted water for about 15 minutes, until *al dente*, adding the broccoli about halfway through.

Meanwhile, heat 3 tablespoons of the olive oil in a large saucepan, and gently fry the garlic and chilli for a few minutes. Add the tomatoes and a splash of white wine.

Add the cleaned mussels to the garlic pan, put the lid on and heat gently until the mussels open, about 8–10 minutes. Discard any mussels that have not opened. When you can handle them, discard the majority of the shells, adding the meat to the sauce.

Drain the pasta and broccoli, and add to the mussels in the saucepan. Mix together well and pour on a little stream of fresh extra virgin olive oil. Serve immediately.

SERVES 4

—350g (12oz) dried *orecchiette* pasta
—500g (1lb 2oz) small broccoli florets
—salt and freshly ground black pepper

SAUCE
—1kg (2lb 4oz) live mussels
—extra virgin olive oil
—2 garlic cloves, peeled and chopped
—1 small chilli, chopped
—8 cherry tomatoes, halved
—a splash of white wine

## CRAUTI FRESCO
### *Fresh Sauerkraut*

There is a part of Italy which, for historical and geographical reasons, is culturally bound to Austria. The food specialities here in the north-east of Italy, in areas like the Tyrol and Alto Adige, are very Germanic indeed, but have been adopted by the Italians. *Crauti*, as the Italians call *sauerkraut*, can be made fresh using Savoy cabbage, as I describe below, or you can use either the fermented one sold in jars or the white cabbage served from wooden tubs at the market, and make either of them more interesting with some flavourful additions, again as below.

Heat the olive oil in a large saucepan, and fry the leek and the speck (if using) for a few minutes. Add the cabbage and the apple juice and cook for a few more minutes. Add the vinegar and sugar and cook gently to soften, adding a little water if necessary, for at least 15 minutes. Taste to see if it is all cooked and flavourful enough, if not add salt and pepper to taste.

Serve as a vegetable accompaniment for sausages or other pork dishes.

SERVES 6

- —4 tablespoons extra virgin olive oil
- —1 medium leek, cleaned and cut into small rounds
- —50g (1¾oz) *speck*, cut into small cubes (optional)
- —800g (1lb 12oz) Savoy cabbage (only the white internal part), very finely chopped
- —150ml (5fl oz/⅔ cup) cloudy apple juice
- —2 tablespoons white wine vinegar
- —1 tablespoon caster sugar (superfine sugar)
- —salt and freshly ground black pepper

*brassicas*

## CRAUTI
### *Sauerkraut*

The cabbage you buy in a jar or from a tub in the market is fermented *sauerkraut*, which means that it has been sitting, weighted down, in its salty tub for quite some time. The flavour, once the ferment is complete, is slightly sour, which you can modify by adding orange or apple juice, juniper berries, etc.

Heat the olive oil in a large saucepan, and fry the onion for about 10 minutes to soften. Add the juniper berries, cumin seeds, *sauerkraut*, apples and apple juice. Bring to the boil and cook over a gentle heat for 30–40 minutes. Season to taste with salt and pepper.

Serve with boiled or roast pork. It's a great dish for vegetarians, just eaten with bread.

SERVES 4–6

—3 tablespoons extra virgin olive oil
—1 small onion, peeled and finely chopped
—15 juniper berries
—1 teaspoon cumin seeds
—1 x 1.5kg (3lb 5oz) jar of *sauerkraut*, or 1.5kg (3lb 5oz) ready-made from a tub
—2 fresh apples, cored and finely grated
—1 litre (1¾ pints / 4 cups) apple juice
—salt and freshly ground black pepper

## CAPONNET
### *Baked Cabbage Parcels*

These little parcels form a part of many a celebratory *antipasto* spread in the north of Italy. The filling can be made from any meat, whether fresh like *lucanica* sausage or leftover roast meat. The only thing that is mandatory is Savoy cabbage, which forms the traditional wrapping. Use the second layer of leaves, as the outer layer will probably be too tough. My mother was very good at making these, and they were a must in our family during autumn and winter.

First of all, blanch the Savoy cabbage leaves in lightly salted boiling water for 5 minutes. This makes them flexible. Drain and lay out on a clean tea-towel to dry. If the central stalk is tough, cut it out.

Preheat the oven to 160°C (325°F/gas 3).

If using fresh sausage, remove from its casing and crumble into a bowl. Very finely chop any roast meats or other meats, and add to the bowl. Add the eggs, breadcrumbs, garlic, chilli (if using), a couple of grates of nutmeg and the Parmesan. Add salt and pepper to taste, and mix well.

Divide the filling mixture between the cabbage leaves. Fold the leaves up around the filling to make parcels, and secure with a wooden cocktail stick.

Lay the little parcels on a baking tray, dot with the butter and sprinkle with the Parmesan. Bake in the preheated oven for 20 minutes, and serve hot or cold.

SERVES 4

— 8 Savoy cabbage leaves
— 25g (1oz) unsalted butter
— 15g (½oz) Parmesan, freshly grated
— salt and freshly ground black pepper

FILLING
— 300g (10½oz) meat (my favourite is a combination of 100g/3½oz fresh sausage meat and 200g/7oz leftover roast meat)
— 2 medium eggs, beaten
— 2 tablespoons fresh white or brown breadcrumbs
— 2 garlic cloves, peeled and crushed
— a pinch of dried chilli (optional)
— freshly grated nutmeg
— 50g (1¾oz) Parmesan, freshly grated

*brassicas*

# RIBOLLITA
*Tuscan Bean and Cabbage Soup*

'Ribollita' means re-boiled, and that is exactly what happens with this classic Tuscan soup: it is made a day or two in advance, then reheated, when it tastes better. It is a peasant soup, originally made from leftovers, or whatever was in season. There are many variations, but all contain cabbage and other vegetables, bread and cannellini beans.

Soak the cannellini beans overnight in cold water to cover. The next day drain the beans, and cover with 2 litres (3 ½ pints/8 cups) of fresh water in a saucepan. Bring to the boil for 10 minutes, then cook for 2 hours, or until tender. Using a slotted spoon, lift out half the soft beans and blitz them to a purée in a blender. Add back to the whole beans and their broth.

Meanwhile, trim the cabbage, cutting away the stalks from the cavolo nero, and the thick stalks from the Savoy. You are using the leaves only. Shred the leaves.

Heat 50ml (2fl oz/3½ tablespoons) of olive oil in a large saucepan and cook the leeks, carrot and celery for 10 minutes. Add the garlic, potatoes, courgettes, cabbage and chopped tomatoes, then cover and cook very gently for an hour.

Add the thyme and the beans with their broth to the pan, and gently cook for a further 30 minutes. When everything is soft, add salt and pepper to taste. Leave overnight now, if you like.

To serve, warm the soup through thoroughly for about 20 minutes. Toast or grill the slices of bread, and put a slice in each bowl. Pour the soup on top. Drizzle with extra virgin olive oil, and grind on lots of black pepper. Eat warm.

SERVES 6

—300g (10½oz) dried *cannellini* beans
—600g (1lb 5oz) *cavolo nero* or outer Savoy cabbage leaves
—extra virgin olive oil
—2 leeks, finely sliced
—1 large carrot, diced
—2 celery stalks, diced
—2 garlic cloves, peeled and sliced
—2 large potatoes, peeled and diced
—2 courgettes (zucchini), diced
—1 x 400g (14oz) tin of chopped tomatoes
—1 sprig of fresh thyme
—salt and freshly ground black pepper

TO SERVE
—6 slices good Italian bread, preferably day-old

# FRITELLE DI CAVOLFIORE
*Cauliflower Fritters*

Not so long ago I managed to cook for my five grandchildren when they were visiting me. They were very fond of this simple recipe, which is good to eat at any time.

Cook the cauliflower in boiling salted water until soft, about 10 minutes. Drain.

Put the eggs, flour and chives into a large bowl, and season with salt and pepper to taste. Mix well together to form a batter, then add the cauliflower florets, and stir.

Add enough olive oil to a medium frying pan so it is 3cm (1¼ inches) deep. Place over a medium heat. To test whether the oil has reached the perfect frying temperature, drop a small piece of bread in. If it fries and goes golden, the oil is ready.

Take a tablespoon of the cauliflower mixture and drop it into the oil. If there is room, add another tablespoonful of the mixture to the pan – you will have to fry in batches. Fry the little fritters until golden on one side then turn to finish the other side, about 6 minutes altogether. Lift the fritters on to absorbent kitchen paper to drain, while you fry the remaining mixture until it is all used up.

Serve the fritters hot, but they are also very good cold as well.

MAKES 24 FRITTERS

—1 medium cauliflower, divided into small florets
—olive oil, for shallow-frying
—salt and freshly ground black pepper

BATTER
—3 medium eggs, beaten
—3 tablespoons plain flour (all-purpose flour)
—2 tablespoons finely chopped fresh chives

## CAVOLO RAPA AL BURRO E CERFOGLIO
*Kohlrabi with Butter and Chervil*

This is a very curious vegetable indeed, like a cross between a turnip and a giant radish, looking like a Sputnik. This delicate-tasting green bulb can bring great pleasure to the last days of winter and the first days of spring. Use as a side dish or a first course.

Cut the quartered kohlrabi into smaller pieces. Melt the butter in a frying pan, and add the kohlrabi pieces along with a little water. Cook at a low temperature for as long as it takes for the kohlrabi to become *al dente* soft, and for the water to disappear, probably up to about 10 minutes (but depending on the size of the pieces).

Add a pinch of paprika, some salt and pepper to taste, and the finely chopped herbs. Mix well, and serve hot.

SERVES 4

—2 large kohlrabi, about 700g (1lb 9oz), peeled and quartered
—80g (2¾oz) unsalted butter
—1 teaspoon paprika
—2 tablespoons each of finely chopped fresh chervil and chives
—salt and freshly ground black pepper

# TIANO DI CAVOLINI
## *Brussels Sprouts Gratin*

Brussels sprouts are not used that much in Italy but do appear occasionally in the northern regions. They eat a lot of cabbage there, and Brussels, of course, belong to the same Brassica family. I think they are the shoot vegetable 'par excellence'.

Cook the Brussels sprouts in salted water until nearly soft, about 4 minutes. Drain.

Preheat the oven to 180°C (350°F/Gas 4).

Make the cheese sauce. Melt the butter in a medium pan, then add the flour. Stir until the flour has amalgamated with the butter. Now start adding the milk gradually, stirring all the time. Bring to the boil, still stirring, to avoid lumps forming. When thick, add some nutmeg and pepper, all the Fontina, and 50g (1¾oz) of the Parmesan. Stir to a smooth sauce. Taste for salt, though you shouldn't need it.

Put the cooked and drained sprouts into an ovenproof dish, and pour the cheese sauce over them. Sprinkle with the remaining Parmesan. Bake in the preheated oven for 20 minutes, and serve as an accompaniment to meat or fish, or as a first course.

SERVES 6

—600g (1lb 5oz) Brussels sprouts, well trimmed
—salt and freshly ground black pepper

CHEESE SAUCE
—50g (1¾oz) unsalted butter
—25g (1oz) plain flour (all-purpose flour)
—500ml (18fl oz/2 cups) milk, warmed
—freshly grated nutmeg
—100g (3½oz) Fontina cheese, freshly grated
—70g (2½oz) Parmesan, freshly grated

## INSALATA DI RINFORZO
*Pickled Christmas Salad*

This typical Neapolitan dish is made around Christmas time, and a bowlful is usually positioned strategically, where there is most traffic, prior to a mealtime. The idea is to pick up a piece of pickled vegetable in your fingers as you pass, in order to stimulate appetite. I have been known to pass so often, that I am full before I even sit down…

Prepare the vegetables first.

Pour the vinegar into a large saucepan and add 2 litres (3½ pints/8 cups) of water and the salt. When boiling, add all the vegetables and the olives, and cook until *al dente* (with a little bite), or softer if you prefer.

Drain off the liquid, then season and lightly coat the cooked vegetables with some extra virgin olive oil. Put into a ceramic bowl, and leave in a spot where they will be most appreciated.

SERVES 6–8

—1 cauliflower, divided into chunks or small florets
—200g (7oz) carrots, peeled and cut into little chunks
—2 large red or yellow peppers, deseeded and cut into strips
—100g (3½oz) small onions, peeled
—1 litre (1¾ pints/4 cups) white wine vinegar
—30g (1oz) table salt
—100g (3½oz) pitted black olives
—extra virgin olive oil

*brassicas*

## SOFFIATO DI CAVOLO NERO CON SALSA DI ACCIUGHE
### *Black Cabbage Soufflé with Anchovy Sauce*

MOF, MOF (which means 'minimum of fuss, maximum of flavour') is my motto, but it does not apply in this recipe, which requires a little more attention. There is, however, considerable compensation in the resulting incredible flavour. It will also attest to your cooking expertise – for soufflés are not easy...

Cut the black cabbage leaves and stalks into smaller pieces, and boil in slightly salted water for 10–12 minutes. Drain, then, when cool enough to handle, squeeze out any excess water. Put into a blender.

Make a thick béchamel sauce by melting 80g (2¾oz) of the butter in a saucepan. Add the flour, and stir to amalgamate the flour with the melted butter. Add the warmed milk slowly, stirring constantly to avoid lumps, until the sauce is very thick. Stir in the Parmesan, salt, pepper and cayenne pepper. Remove from the heat.

Preheat the oven to 200°C (400°F/gas 6). Use the remaining butter to grease the inside of six small ramekins.

In a roomy bowl, beat the egg whites until stiff.

Add the béchamel sauce and the egg yolks to the leaves in the blender, then process until smooth. Pour into a bowl. Into this carefully fold the egg white, using a metal spoon.

Pour the mixture into the buttered ramekins to come three-quarters of the way up the sides. Place on a baking sheet, and bake in the preheated oven for 13–14 minutes. The mixture should rise over the rim of the ramekin, and turn brown.

Serve by making an incision in the top and pouring some *bagna cauda* into it. Delicious!

SERVES 4–6

—2–3 leaves and stalks of *cavolo nero*, about 90g (3¼oz)
—120g (4¼oz) unsalted butter
—80g (2¾oz/⅓ cup) self-raising flour
—about 400ml (14fl oz/1¾ cups) milk, warmed
—80g (2¾oz) Parmesan, freshly grated
—½ teaspoon cayenne pepper
—3 medium eggs, separated
—salt and freshly ground pepper

TO SERVE
— *bagna cauda* (see page 166)

# FRITTATA DI PISELLI E CARCIOFI
*Pea and Artichoke Omelette*

If you cook onions and peas together, you will have a sauce for pasta or rice, such as the *risi e bisi* from Venice. But by adding artichokes, you can create the base for this wonderful *frittata*, to be eaten as a starter or main course.

Put the onion, peas, artichokes and half the olive oil into a non-stick saucepan and add a little water, about 50ml (2fl oz/¼ cup). Cook until the water has evaporated and the peas are cooked to your liking.

Beat the eggs in a large bowl, and stir in the vegetables, the Parmesan, mint and some salt and pepper to taste.

Heat a little of the remaining oil in a 25cm (10 inch) frying pan, then add the egg mixture. Cook gently, to let it solidify on one side, about 10 minutes. Every now and again use a spatula to gently loosen the base of the omelette from the sides, which allows some of the liquid mixture to hit the base of the pan and set. When there is no more liquid left, put a plate over the top of the pan and invert the omelette on to the plate, then slide it back into the pan, uncooked side down. Add the remaining oil, and brown the other side, about 5–6 minutes.

Serve hot or cold.

SERVES 4–6

—1 large onion, peeled and finely sliced
—200g (7oz) fresh podded garden peas (frozen allowed)
—4 little artichoke hearts, cut into slices
—8 tablespoons extra virgin olive oil
—10 medium eggs
—30g (1oz) Parmesan, freshly grated
—2 tablespoons chopped fresh mint
—salt and freshly ground black pepper

*pods and seeds*

## PANISSA
### *Beans and Pork with Rice*

Vercelli and Novara, two cities in Piedmont, are where this dish is a speciality. It is very pleasant, designed to satisfy the hunger of working people. It used to be made with locally produced ingredients – the pork and beans best from Saluggia, and the rice from the Po Valley. Preferably you should use cooking sausages, ones for boiling, as they need to cook for a long time in this recipe.

Heat the olive oil in a large saucepan and fry the onion until soft, about 10 minutes. Add the sausages and brown them on each side.

Drain the soaked beans, add to the sausage pan, and cover everything with water. Bring to the boil, then lower the heat, cover and simmer for 1¹/₂ hours. Add more water if necessary during this time. When cooked, drain.

Put the stock in a suitable pot on the stove, next to where you are working, and keep it hot.

Now stir the rice into the beans pan, and work as for a risotto, adding hot boiling stock, a ladle at a time, as the previous ladleful is absorbed. Cook until the rice is *al dente* – probably about 15–20 minutes. It should not be too wet.

Cut the sausages into pieces and return to the rice and beans. Season to taste, and serve sprinkled with grated Parmesan.

SERVES 6

—4 tablespoons extra virgin olive oil
—1 onion, peeled and finely chopped
—6 pure pork, semi-dry Italian sausages, skins removed (or regular plain pork sausages, skin on)
—300g (10¹/₂oz) dried *Saluggia* or *borlotti* beans, soaked in water for 24 hours and then drained
—1.5 litres (2³/₄ pints / 6 cups) good chicken or vegetable stock
—300g (10¹/₂oz / 1¹/₂ cups) *carnaroli* or *arborio* risotto rice
—salt and freshly ground black pepper
—freshly grated Parmesan, to serve

# PASTA E FASULI
*Pasta and Bean Soup*

*Fasuli* is the Neapolitan argot for *fagioli* or beans, and this pasta and bean soup almost doesn't need an introduction because it is so well-known worldwide in restaurants, cafés and *trattorie*. It is a peasant dish that reigns supreme, and there are as many versions as there are regions in Italy, possibly even more! But they basically use the same method, cooking beans and pasta together with some flavouring, perhaps meaty, perhaps herby. This one is for vegetarians, with no meat, but, if you were tempted, you could fry 50g (1¾oz) of Parma ham cubes in a little oil until crisp, and serve them on top…

If using dried *borlotti*, soak the beans overnight, then drain. Cover the fresh beans or the drained dried beans with 2 litres (3½ pints/8 cups) of water and bring to the boil. Cook at a simmer until soft, which will be about an hour for the fresh beans, double that for the dried beans.

Heat 5 tablespoons of olive oil in a large saucepan and fry the onion gently for 10 minutes, until soft. Add the basil, rosemary, chilli and tomato paste, and simmer for 10 minutes. Add the soft beans and their water (or the tinned beans and the stock), as well as the pasta, then cover and cook for about 10 minutes, until the pasta is cooked. Season with salt and pepper, and drizzle a little extra virgin olive oil on top.

SERVES 6

— 300g (10½oz) fresh podded *borlotti* beans, or 200g (7oz) dried *borlotti*, soaked overnight in water and then drained (or 3 x 400g/14oz tins of cooked *borlotti* beans, drained)
— extra virgin olive oil
— 1 small onion, peeled and finely chopped
— 2 tablespoons fresh basil leaves
— 1 sprig of fresh rosemary
— 1 red chilli, finely chopped
— 1 tablespoon tomato paste
— 1 litre (1¾ pints/4 cups) chicken or vegetable stock (only if using tinned beans)
— 150g (5½oz) mixed pasta, small shapes preferably
— salt and freshly ground black pepper

# FAVE E PROSCIUTTO
*Braised Broad Beans and Ham*

A very simple broad bean (fava bean) dish, which uses the youngest and freshest of beans – ideally those you grow yourself. If the beans are a little older, the internal skin is too tough, and you won't be able to use the pods. I have to admit that until now I have always discarded the pods of broad beans, wasting four-fifths of the vegetable. But if you pluck your own pods from the garden, both pods and beans are deliciously edible.

Eat the beans by themselves with bread, or as a side dish for meat, game or pork. In the extreme you can also use frozen beans (but no pods, and you might have to take off the outer grey-green skin).

Take the beans out of the pods, keeping the pods. Top and tail the pods, and cut them into small cubes.

Put the olive oil into a large frying pan, and fry the onions gently until soft, about 10 minutes. Add the broad beans, the pod cubes and 125ml (4fl oz/½ cup) of water, and cook gently until tender, about another 10 minutes.

Add the ham, salt and pepper to taste, and serve hot.

SERVES 4

—600g (1lb 5oz) very young broad beans (fava beans) in their pods
—4 tablespoons extra virgin olive oil
—2 medium white onions, peeled and finely sliced
—100g (3½oz) cooked ham, cut into small cubes
—salt and freshly ground black pepper

*pods and seeds*

# FAGIOLINI BIANCHI AL PANGRATTATO
*Wax Beans with Butter and Breadcrumbs*

For this simple dish, I use wax beans, which cook in the same way and look similar to green beans, but they are creamy white in colour. They are wonderful used in salads, but this particular dish can be used as a side dish or as a starter.

Boil the wax beans in salted water until soft, about 10–12 minutes.

Meanwhile, prepare the toasted breadcrumbs. Heat the butter in a small pan until foaming, then add the breadcrumbs and salt and pepper to taste. Stir-fry until the breadcrumbs are golden.

Drain the beans and place on serving plates. Top with a quarter of the breadcrumbs per portion.

SERVES 4

—600g (1lb 5oz) wax beans, topped and tailed
—70g (2½oz / ¾ cup) dried white breadcrumbs
—30g (1oz) unsalted butter
—salt and freshly ground black pepper

## TACCOLE AL POMODORO E PATATE
*Braised Tomatoes, Mangetout and Potatoes*

A delightful soup-starter, which has to be accompanied by bread. With less watery tomatoes it can also be served as a side dish to chicken or even fish.

Heat the olive oil in a medium saucepan and fry the garlic for a few minutes. Add the tomatoes and the potatoes with a little water, and cook for about 15 minutes, until the potatoes are almost cooked.

Add the mangetout, basil, and salt and pepper to taste, and continue cooking gently. Serve when the mangetout are cooked to your liking.

SERVES 4

—4 tablespoons extra virgin olive oil
—2 garlic cloves, peeled and finely chopped
—2 large tomatoes, roughly chopped, or 1 x 400g (14oz) tin of chopped tomatoes
—300g (10½oz) small new potatoes, washed but unpeeled
—500g (1lb 2oz) mangetout (snow peas) or sugar snaps, topped and tailed
—2 tablespoons torn fresh basil leaves
—salt and freshly ground black pepper

*pods and seeds*

This is a recipe I adapted from a German recipe called *Birnen, Bohnen und Speck,* where I substitute neck of lamb for the pork belly. It is a really remarkable combination of lamb, vegetables and fruit.

Put the lamb, garlic and onions into a heavy saucepan large enough to contain them, and cover with cold water. Bring to the boil, then turn down the heat and simmer gently until you see the meat separating from the bone. This should take about 1½–2 hours.

If there is any fat on the top of the stew, spoon it off and discard.

Add the beans, along with the pears and oregano, to the stew. Season with salt and pepper to taste, and cook until the pears are soft, about 15–20 minutes.

Serve the meat, beans and pears with a little of their stock. Some plainly boiled potatoes would make a good accompaniment.

SERVES 4

—2 x 500g (1lb 2oz) meaty lamb necks, still on the bone
—4 garlic cloves, peeled and chopped
—2 small onions, peeled and sliced
—400g (14oz) green beans, topped and cut in half
—4 large firm pears, peeled, quartered and cored
—1 small sprig of fresh oregano
—salt and freshly ground black pepper

*pods and seeds*

## FAGIOLI DI SOIA CON TONNO E CIPOLLA
*Edamame Beans with Tuna and Onion*

Soya beans have became a major and important addition to the Italian agricultural economy. This is a classic recipe, usually made with *borlotti* beans. Soya beans are not usually available fresh, but you can find them frozen, labelled as edamame beans, which are immature soya beans. (Edamame beans are often found in the pod, but you want unpadded ones for this recipe.)

Should the onions be too strong in flavour for you, soak them in water for 30 minutes. Drain and slice very finely.

Boil the beans in water for 8 minutes, or longer if from frozen. Drain well.

Break the tuna into smaller chunks and put into a serving bowl, then add the onions and drained beans. Season to taste with salt and pepper.

Mix together the olive oil and lemon juice, and season to taste with salt and pepper. Use this to dress the salad. Decorate with the celery leaves and lemon wedges and serve as an *antipasto* with some good country bread.

SERVES 4

—4–6 salad or large spring onions
—500g (1lb 2oz) edamame beans (frozen will do)
—200g (7oz) good tinned tuna in oil (preferably *ventresca di tonno*, the very tender belly of the tuna), drained
—6 tablespoons extra virgin olive oil
—juice of 1 lemon, plus extra wedges to serve
—2 tablespoons chopped celery leaves
—salt and freshly ground black pepper

# FRITTEDDA
## *Sicilian Springtime Stew*

This dish, a stew of seasonal vegetables, is just wonderful, provided you find the right ingredients at the right time. The best months in Italy are March and April, which obviously vary by location. The Sicilians eat it as an inviting starter.

This is indeed very simple. Put all the vegetables, plus the parsley and capers, into a casserole with a lid. Add the olive oil and a little water to come halfway up the vegetables, and cook gently for 20 minutes with the lid on. Taste for salt and pepper.

Eat with *panelle* (see page 203).

SERVES 4–6

— 600g (1lb 5oz) small, tender artichokes, trimmed of tougher leaves and halved
— 400g (14oz) young white onions, peeled and sliced
— 300g (10½oz) podded garden peas
— 300g (10½oz) podded, very young broad beans (fava beans)
— 4 tablespoons coarsely chopped fresh flat-leaf parsley
— 1 tablespoon salted capers, desalted (see page 75) and chopped
— 100ml (3½fl oz/scant ½ cup) extra virgin olive oil
— salt and freshly ground black pepper

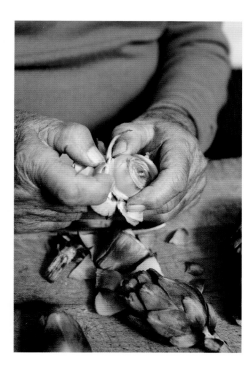

# CARCIOFI RIPIENI
## *Stuffed Artichokes*

For this dish you need those wonderful Italian artichokes, not too big, but with spines on top (they are tastier), which come from Puglia, Sicily or Sardinia. The tenderest ones will have a small choke inside and are delicious to eat whole when the outer leaves and the tops have been discarded.

To desalt the capers, soak them in a bowl of cold water for 15 minutes, then drain well before using.

For the stuffing, put the breadcrumbs into a bowl. Add enough milk to moisten them, then squeeze out any excess milk. Add the capers, garlic, parsley, egg yolks, olive oil and a little salt and pepper to the breadcrumbs. Mix everything together to a soft paste.

Open the tops of the artichokes with your fingers and make space for the filling. Use a small spoon to fill the hole in each artichoke with the stuffing mixture.

Place the artichokes tightly next to each other in a casserole or other stove-top braising dish. Pour over the 125ml (4fl oz/½ cup) of olive oil and top up with boiling water to raise the level to 1cm (½ inch) from the top of the artichokes. Cover with the lid, and place on the stove. Bring to the boil, then reduce the heat and cook for 35 minutes, until the artichokes are tender. Test this by inserting the point of a sharp knife.

Eat the artichokes either by themselves as a first course, or to accompany meat or fish dishes. They can be served hot or cold.

SERVES 8

—24 small fresh artichokes, trimmed and cleaned, removing any choke
—125ml (4fl oz/½ cup) extra virgin olive oil

STUFFING
—150g (5½oz/3 cups) fresh white breadcrumbs
—4 tablespoons milk
—1 tablespoon salted capers, desalted (see above) and chopped
—2 garlic cloves, peeled and crushed
—2 tablespoons coarsely chopped fresh flat-leaf parsley
—2 medium egg yolks
—2 tablespoons extra virgin olive oil
—salt and freshly ground black pepper

*stalks and shoots*

# CARCIOFINI SOTT'OLIO
*Pickled Artichokes in Oil*

One of the most sought-after items in an Italian *antipasto* are *carciofini sott'olio*. You will need to find the smallest artichokes, which in Italy are specially sold for this purpose. The tiniest artichokes are those that grow up the stalk of the plant, and can be compared to the cabbage shoots we know as Brussels sprouts. In fact that gives me an idea…

You will need one large jar, or a couple of smaller ones. These need to be well sterilized before use. Put them through a dishwasher cycle, or in a low oven for about 20 minutes.

—1.5kg (3lb 5oz) very small artichokes (*carciofini*)
—1 litre (1¾fl oz/4 cups) good, strong white wine vinegar
—50g (1¾oz) salt
—extra virgin olive oil
—freshly ground black pepper

Trim and cut the tougher parts and leaves off the artichokes, leaving only the centres, or hearts, which should be about the size of a walnut.

Pour the vinegar into a large saucepan, and add the salt and 200ml (7fl oz/just over ¾ cup) of water. Bring to the boil, then add the artichokes, turn the heat down, and cook for 30–40 minutes, making sure they are well cooked in the centre.

Drain the artichokes, but take care not to touch them with your hands. Put to cool on a very clean cloth. When they are well cooled, take a sterile spoon and, one by one, put them into the sterilized jar with a twist of black pepper. Add some oil and continue to fill the jar with artichoke hearts, pepper and olive oil. Finally, cover with olive oil, seal with a lid and label.

Keep for a couple of months in a cool place. When opened, try to eat them relatively quickly. Be aware that if you put them in the refrigerator, the oil tends to congeal. This is normal and disappears at room temperature.

FILLS 1 X 1.5KG (3LB 5OZ) JAR

# PINZIMONIO
## *Crudités with Oil and Vinegar Dip*

One of the most curious eating habits found in the north of Italy, and in Tuscany, is the dipping of various raw and tender vegetables into a little bowl of extra virgin olive oil mixed with some vinegar, salt and pepper. This is served at the beginning of a summer meal, accompanied by fresh crispy bread. The winter equivalent is *bagna cauda,* which comes from Piedmont (see page 166), also a dip for vegetables, but served warm.

Cut all the vegetables into sticks, or as described.

Divide the olive oil between the relevant number of small bowls with the vinegar and salt and pepper to taste. Or serve in one communal bowl.

To eat, dip the vegetables into your own individual bowl, or the communal one, picking up some of the salt and vinegar from the bottom. Serve with good fresh country bread.

SERVES 4–6

—8 young asparagus spears
—8 spring onions, cleaned
—8 small tender carrots
—4 artichoke hearts, quartered
—2 small cucumbers
—4 small celery stalks, halved
—2 fennel bulbs, cut into eighths

DIP
—about 150ml (5fl oz/²⁄₃ cup) extra virgin olive oil
—4–6 teaspoons wine vinegar or balsamic vinegar
—salt and freshly ground black pepper

*stalks and shoots*

**77**

## FRITTATA CON ASPARAGI E CIPOLLE

*Asparagus and Onion Omelette*

This is an ideal dish to take to a picnic, as it is good cold, or it can be served as a starter. Obviously, it could also be served as a main course, but for fewer people.

Cook the asparagus chunks in a little boiling salted water for 10–12 minutes. Drain well.

Heat half the olive oil in a 25cm (10 inch) frying pan and fry the onions until soft but not brown, about 10 minutes. Add the cooked and drained asparagus.

Beat the eggs in a bowl and mix with the cheese, parsley and salt and pepper to taste.

Heat the onion and asparagus pan up well, adding a little more of the remaining oil, then add the egg mixture. Cook gently, to let it solidify on one side, about 10 minutes. Every now and again use a spatula to gently loosen the base of the omelette from the sides, which allows some of the liquid mixture to hit the base of the pan and set. When there is no more liquid left, put a plate over the top of the pan and invert the omelette on to the plate, then slide it back into the pan, uncooked side down. Add the remaining oil, and brown the other side, about 5–6 minutes.

Serve hot or cold.

SERVES 4–6

—1 bunch of green asparagus, each spear peeled, trimmed and cut into 3 pieces
—6 tablespoons extra virgin olive oil
—400g (14oz) white onions, peeled and finely sliced
—10 medium eggs
—50g (1³/₄oz) Parmesan, freshly grated
—2 tablespoons finely chopped fresh flat-leaf parsley
—salt and freshly ground black pepper

## ASPARAGI AL BURRO E PARMIGIANO
*Asparagus with Butter and Parmesan*

One of the simplest ways of eating fresh asparagus in season in Italy is dressing it with melted butter (or the finest olive oil) and freshly grated Parmesan. So simple, in fact, it hardly needs a recipe. In Italy you can get white or green asparagus, the white being more delicate in flavour.

Serve as a starter or light lunch, and if you want the dish to be a little more substantial, you could serve a fried egg on top of the asparagus spears.

—1kg (2lb 4oz) medium asparagus spears, green or white
—60g (2¼oz) unsalted butter, melted
—60g (2¼oz) Parmesan, freshly grated
—salt and freshly ground black pepper

Break the tough ends off the asparagus spears, and peel the lower stems. Cook the spears in slightly salted water for about 15–20 minutes – this is the Italian way, until slightly soft. Drain.

Divide the spears between serving plates, and top with melted butter and a sprinkling of freshly grated Parmesan. Sprinkle also with a little freshly ground black pepper.

Serve with a *soma d'ail* or *bruschetta* (see page 119).

SERVES 4

# ZUPPA DI CARDO E GNOCCHI DI POLLO
*Cardoon Soup with Chicken Dumplings*

The exquisite and delicate taste of the cardoon combines wonderfully with the chicken dumplings, which are also quite delicate in flavour. Sometimes I use the thick white stems of Swiss chard or celery stalks for a similarly pleasant soup. Remember to take the side strings off the stalks of the cardoon.

Put the stock into a suitable saucepan, and heat until boiling. Add the cardoon, garlic and seasonings to taste, and simmer for 30 minutes, until the cardoon is tender. Remove the garlic cloves.

Meanwhile, prepare the chicken dumplings by mixing all the ingredients together well. With your hands, form the mixture into dumplings the size of walnuts.

Add the dumplings to the soup. Cook the soup and dumplings together for another 10–15 minutes. Serve, perhaps with some more grated Parmesan sprinkled on top of the soup.

SERVES 4

—1.5 litres (2¾ pints/6 cups) chicken stock (a cube will do)
—300g (10½oz) cardoon, tender stalks cut into 2.5cm (1 inch) chunks
—2 garlic cloves, unpeeled
—a little freshly grated nutmeg
—salt and freshly ground black pepper

DUMPLINGS
—200g (7oz) minced chicken
—1 garlic clove, peeled and crushed
—a little freshly grated nutmeg
—50g (1¾oz) Parmesan, freshly grated, plus extra to serve
—1 tablespoon fresh flat-leaf parsley, very finely chopped
—4 tablespoons fresh fine white breadcrumbs
—2 medium eggs, beaten

# CARDI AL FORNO
## *Oven-baked Cardoon*

You could also use blanched slices of fennel or celeriac instead of the cardoon. Before cooking the cardoon, it is necessary to take the strings off the surface of the stalks using a sharp knife.

Boil the cardoon in salted water until nearly tender, about 15–20 minutes. Drain well.

Preheat the oven to 200°C (400°F/gas 6).

Arrange the cardoon pieces on a non-stick baking tray so that they look like roof tiles. Sprinkle with the butter, breadcrumbs and cheese. Season with salt, pepper and nutmeg to taste.

Bake in the preheated oven for 15 minutes, or until golden. Serve as a side dish with meat or fish.

SERVES 4

—600g (1lb 5oz) cardoon, tender stalks cut into 7.5cm (3 inch) pieces
—60g (2¼oz) unsalted butter, in small pieces
—60g (2¼oz) dried white breadcrumbs
—60g (2¼oz) Parmesan, freshly grated
—freshly grated nutmeg
—salt and freshly ground black pepper

# LINGUINE CON FINOCCHIO E GAMBERETTI
*Fennel and Prawn Linguine*

This sauce came about by pure chance when I discovered I had only fennel and prawns (shrimp) in the refrigerator. It is very delicate and elegant!

For the sauce, heat the olive oil and butter together in a large frying pan, and fry the shallots gently for 10 minutes. Add the fennel and wine, and cook until the fennel is soft, adding a little water if necessary, about another 10 minutes.

Now cook the pasta in boiling salted water for 6–7 minutes, until *al dente* or as you prefer. Drain well.

Add the peeled prawns to the fennel and cook for 5 minutes, then add salt, plenty of black pepper and the dill. Mix the *linguine* into the sauce, and serve hot.

SERVES 4

—350g (12oz) *linguine* pasta
—salt and freshly ground black pepper

SAUCE
—50ml (2fl oz / ¼ cup) extra virgin olive oil
—50g (1¾oz) unsalted butter
—2 small shallots, peeled and finely chopped
—500g (1lb 2oz) tender central part of fennel bulb, finely chopped
—50ml (2fl oz / ¼ cup) dry white wine
—300g (10½fl oz) fresh, large, peeled prawns (shrimp)
—1 tablespoon finely chopped fresh dill

INSALATA
DI CAMPO
PRIMAVERA
(*Springtime
Field Salad*)
*Page 86*

## INSALATA DI CAMPO PRIMAVERA
### *Springtime Field Salad*

In springtime fields in Italy and France (but rarely in England), you often see people armed with baskets and knives, bending from time to time to collect the new tender growth of dandelion, wild sorrel or wild garlic. It is food for free, and these leaves are all available in the UK!

I traditionally make this salad for Easter, and accompany it with *bruschetta*, slices of toasted *ciabatta*.

Wash and dry all the leaves. Put them into a bowl.

Make the vinaigrette by putting the ingredients into a bowl or jar, and beating or agitating until you have an emulsion.

Now prepare the accompaniments. Make the *bruschette*. Halve the quail's eggs. Drain the anchovies.

Pour the vinaigrette over the leaves in the bowl, and mix. Decorate with the halved quail's eggs and the anchovy fillets, and offer the *bruschette* on the side. Just for fun, you could collect some spring flowers – primroses and violets, for example – and use their petals for decoration as well.

SERVES 4

—150g (5½oz) young dandelion leaves
—50g (1¾oz) young wild sorrel leaves
—100g (3½oz) tender wild garlic leaves
—50g (1¾oz) wild rocket
  (arugula) leaves

VINAIGRETTE
—50ml (2fl oz/¼ cup) extra virgin
  olive oil
—2 tablespoons white wine vinegar or
  balsamic vinegar
—salt and freshly ground black pepper

TO SERVE
—8 slices of *bruschetta* (see page 119)
—12 quail's eggs, hard-boiled
  and peeled
—12 anchovy fillets in oil

# INSALATA VERDE
## *Mixed Green Salad*

Something as simple as a green salad should be an easy affair, but it is not always. Something fresh, crisp and green eaten before a meal prepares the stomach juices to be active, especially if you use good white wine vinegar or lemon juice. The composition of the mixture or leaves is up to you. I usually make the dressing straight on to the salad, and start with the oil first, not with the vinegar and salt, which tend to make the leaves limp. Sometimes a little touch of sugar makes the leaves a little more pleasant, particularly the slightly bitter ones. But you can, of course, make the dressing separately, and mix it well before putting it on the salad.

As a starter eat this salad with *grissini* or bread, and I would not drink wine with it, as the wine does not like the salad's acidity.

Wash all the leaves, and drain them well. To keep them very fresh if not using straight away, put them into a closed plastic bag and keep in the refrigerator until required.

Put the leaves into a large salad bowl.

Mix the olive oil, vinegar, salt, pepper and sugar together in a small bowl or jar. Pour on to the salad and mix well (I do it with my hands). Serve straight away.

SERVES 4

—400g (14oz) green leafy, very fresh salad leaves (baby gem lettuce, watercress, rocket (arugula), young spinach leaves, lamb's lettuce)

VINAIGRETTE
—50ml (2fl oz/ $1/4$ cup) extra virgin olive oil
—2 tablespoons white wine vinegar or the juice of $1/2$ a lemon
—$1/2$ teaspoon caster sugar (superfine sugar)
—salt and freshly ground black pepper

*salad leaves*

# RISOTTO ALL'ACETOSA
*Wild Sorrel Risotto*

The perfect balance of taste between the buttery and creamy rice and the sharpness of the sorrel, particularly the wild version, is sublime. Ideally the rice should be *acquerello carnaroli,* or something of the same high quality, which will be difficult to find. This type of rice cooks in a way unlike any other, presenting the best *al dente* texture.

Put the stock into a suitable pot on the stove, next to where you will make the risotto, and keep it warm.

Heat the olive oil in a large shallow pan, and fry the onion for about 10 minutes, until softened a little. Add the rice and stir around to coat each grain with fat. Now start adding the hot stock in ladlefuls. Start to stir, and as soon as the first lot of liquid is absorbed, add some more, but not enough to drown it. After 5 minutes add some salt and the sorrel leaves, which will dissolve into the rice, giving a nice colour and taste. Continue cooking, stirring and adding stock, for about another 15 minutes, which is when you should taste a grain of rice for your preferred *al dente* texture. Keep the rice moist, but not too wet.

When the rice is to your taste, take the pan off the heat, mix in the Parmesan and the butter, and serve with a sprinkling of freshly ground black pepper.

SERVES 4

— 2 litres (3$^1$/$_2$ pints / 8 cups) hot chicken or vegetable stock
— 3 tablespoons extra virgin olive oil
— 1 medium onion, peeled and finely chopped
— 350g (12oz) *carnaroli* or other good risotto rice
— 200g (7oz) fresh sorrel leaves, tough stems removed
— 50g (1³/₄oz) Parmesan, freshly grated
— 60g (2¹/₄oz) unsalted butter
— salt and freshly ground black pepper

# INSALATA DI DUE RADICCHI CON SPECK
*Two Radicchio Salad*

This is a delightful salad from the Veneto region, where in season you can find the *radicchi* of Treviso, Chioggia and Castelfranco, three quite different-looking vegetables. I am using the Treviso *radicchio* in this recipe because it is the most commonly available. Its salad companion is the long-leaved Belgian chicory. One type of Treviso is also available much later in the year, up to December, which makes it very special in terms of flavour and availability. *Tardivo* means 'the late one', and the *tardivo di Treviso*, with its stronger bitter accents, can be grilled, steamed, roasted, used in a salad… they even make a grappa out of it!

Trim and clean the leaves. Cut both types of leaf into 5cm (2 inch) chunks. Put these chunks into a large bowl, and mix with the *speck*.

Mix the vinaigrette ingredients together in a jar or bowl, and dress the salad. Mix well, and serve as a starter or a side salad. It is especially delicious served with a good dark bread from the area.

SERVES 4–6

—1 large head of *radicchio di Treviso*, about 250g (9oz)
—1 medium head of Belgian chicory, about 250g (9oz)
—70g (2½oz) lean *speck*, cut into small julienne

VINAIGRETTE
—5 tablespoons extra virgin olive oil
—3 tablespoons balsamic vinegar
—½ teaspoon caster sugar (superfine sugar)
—salt and freshly ground black pepper

ROOT VEGETABLES

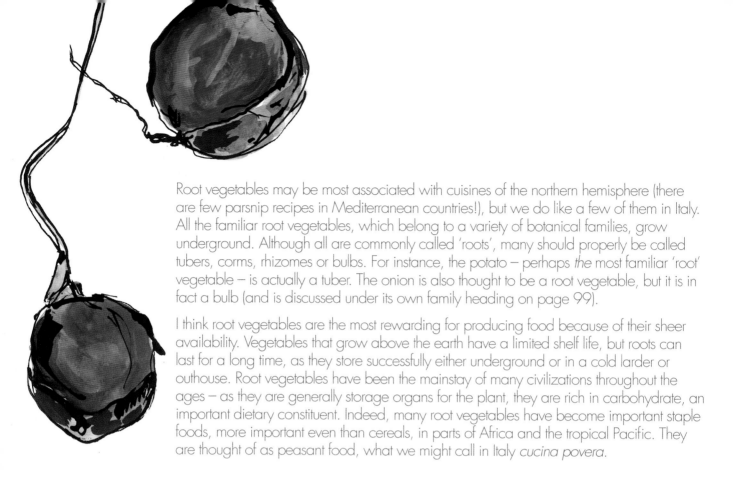

Root vegetables may be most associated with cuisines of the northern hemisphere (there are few parsnip recipes in Mediterranean countries!), but we do like a few of them in Italy. All the familiar root vegetables, which belong to a variety of botanical families, grow underground. Although all are commonly called 'roots', many should properly be called tubers, corms, rhizomes or bulbs. For instance, the potato – perhaps *the* most familiar 'root' vegetable – is actually a tuber. The onion is also thought to be a root vegetable, but it is in fact a bulb (and is discussed under its own family heading on page 99).

I think root vegetables are the most rewarding for producing food because of their sheer availability. Vegetables that grow above the earth have a limited shelf life, but roots can last for a long time, as they store successfully either underground or in a cold larder or outhouse. Root vegetables have been the mainstay of many civilizations throughout the ages – as they are generally storage organs for the plant, they are rich in carbohydrate, an important dietary constituent. Indeed, many root vegetables have become important staple foods, more important even than cereals, in parts of Africa and the tropical Pacific. They are thought of as peasant food, what we might call in Italy *cucina povera*.

## TRUE ROOTS

True root vegetables grow underground and are formed of the main or tap root of the plant – the very first root that the seed puts out – through which moisture and nutrients are absorbed from the surrounding earth. All these true roots are single plants that form only one vegetable, and they include beetroots/beet, carrots, parsnips, radishes, turnips, swedes, salsify/scorzonera and horseradish. They have leaves that grow above ground, some of which can also be eaten – beetroot, carrot, turnip (like my beloved *cime di rapa*) and radish leaves, for instance.

**Beetroot** (*barbabietola*) is a true root, which forms a rounded rather than long tapering shape. It is a vegetable we associate more with northern countries – particularly with Russia and its famous *borscht* – but it has found its way into Italian cooking from time to time. Most beetroots are a deep crimson in colour, although some are golden and white, and an Italian variety has red and white stripes! My mother used to buy beetroot ready cooked, and dress slices with oil, lemon and parsley; I love it as a salad with coriander, which is not very Italian, I admit, but tasty. Boil or bake (in foil) in the oven – or, best of all, in the ashes of a bonfire. One of the sweetest of vegetables, it is baked in cream in the Aosta Valley, and in béchamel sauce in Emilia-Romagna; it is layered with vegetables and fish in a Ligurian fast-day speciality called *cappon magro*. Beetroot is also used for colouring pasta – although I can never detect any beetroot taste – and for a vegetarian *lasagna* (see page 104). The leaves, dark green with crimson veins, are sometimes sold in Italian markets on their own, and can be added to soup, cooked like spinach or Swiss chard. As with many similar leaves, beet leaves can be cooked and mixed with ricotta cheese to make a delicious *ravioli* filling. Thin slices of beetroot can be deep-fried as crisps.

**Carrot** (*carota*) is another true root. The first wild carrots were actually white and spindly, and early attempts at cultivation produced roots in red, purple and black (they weren't popular; I wonder why). It was probably the Dutch who developed the familiar orange colour, as recently as the seventeenth century. Carrots are sweet, flavourful, and packed with goodness, particularly vitamin A, which is good for the eyes. There is an old Italian joke about why horses don't wear glasses: because they eat lots of carrots!

Carrots are one of the few root vegetables that can be eaten raw: in Italy we halve young ones and use them as a crudité with dips (particularly *bagna cauda*), or whole in a *bollito misto*; we grate older carrots for salads, or juice them. They are used as an accompanying vegetable or starter – steamed or sautéed usually, not boiled. But it is as a 'foundation' vegetable that carrots are most appreciated. They are an essential ingredient, along with onion and celery, in the Italian *battuto* and *soffritto*, which form the basis of many meat sauces, and play a major role in many classic soups, stocks and stews. In Italy we pickle carrots in a delicious mix called *giardiniera*, and we also have a delicious cake made from carrots (see page 109)...

**Parsnip** (*pastinaca* or *pastinache*), another true root, is not used much in Italy, although I believe it is fed to the appreciative pigs of Parma! I have grown to love it, though, while living in England. It is delicious roasted with beef on a Sunday, I have had an interesting bread made with grated raw parsnip, and it makes a good vegetable purée and soup. Apparently, before the arrival of the potato, it was a primary source of edible starch in the European diet.

I think **turnip** (*rapa*), another true root, is a lovely vegetable. Its tap root actually fattens into a bulb shape underground, and these roots come in two sizes and seasons: early small turnips are white, shaded purple (looking very like a close relative, radish); main-crop turnips arrive in winter, and look more like another relative, swede. Small bulbs can be grated to eat raw, or they can be braised with butter, and baked with

cheese. Larger, coarser turnips can be fibrous, and more bitter in flavour, but they too cook well – usually to a purée – after peeling. The leaves of turnips can be eaten, but these are not the true *cime di rape* (see Brassicas, page 21).

The **swede** (*rapa svedese*) is closely related to the turnip, and it acquired the name 'swede' because it was grown, possibly developed, in Sweden in the seventeenth century. (It was transplanted to the USA, where it became known as 'rutabaga', Swedish dialect for 'red bags'!) We don't cook much with this large, rather coarse root in Italy, but it is a good puréeing vegetable, known mainly as the 'neeps' (from *napus*, turnip) of Scotland, served with haggis on Burns' Night.

**Scorzonera** and **salsify** (*scorzonera*) are both long and tapering true roots: both have a white flesh, but salsify (also known as oyster plant or vegetable oyster) has a pale skin, while scorzonera has a black skin (the translation of the name from Italian, thus its alternate name of black salsify). We only know scorzonera in Italy, and I find the vegetable quite strange because when peeled it becomes very sticky. The roots may be steamed, boiled, baked or sautéed, or used in soups.

The **radish** (*ravanello*) is one of the few true root vegetables that is most commonly eaten raw. Radishes come in different shapes, from bulbous to long, and in different colours, but are all hot in flavour, and very refreshing. I love to use them in salads and *antipasto* plates.

**Horseradish** is another true root (known as *cren*, *kreen* or *rafano*), which grows in the wild all over Italy (and much of northern Europe). It is not eaten like other roots, as a vegetable, but is more of a seasoning, as it is incredibly hot and pungent in flavour. In fact, when peeling or grating a root raw (the only way you can utilize it), you must wear glasses or goggles, as the juices will irritate your eyes. Horseradish is much used in the north of Italy, where it accompanies all sort of pork dishes. My all-time favourite is a smoked Eastern European sausage called *debreziner*, boiled and served with freshly grated horseradish. Grated raw, horseradish is mixed with cream as a condiment in the UK with roast beef, but it is good with smoked fish as well.

# OTHER ROOTS

The 'root' vegetables described here all grow underground, as do true roots, but they are not tap roots. They are instead underground *stems*, and include tubers, corms and rhizomes.

Tubers are enlarged stems of a plant, rather than enlarged roots, and they grow in thickness rather than in length. Each tuber is a storage organ for the plant and, because it has 'eyes', it can reproduce underground, making new plants (true roots cannot do this). The **potato** (*patata*) is a tuber, and although we think it has been around for ever, it has only been known in the West since the Columbian Exchange of the sixteenth century, when Spanish explorers brought back tomatoes, potatoes, capsicums, turkeys, cocoa, tobacco, etc. from the newly discovered Americas, and introduced in return horses, pigs, etc. *to* the Americas). It was to become the basic, almost sole, crop in Ireland – where little else would grow successfully – and when potato blight attacked in 1845–6, the country was devastated, and at least a million people died, with another million emigrating.

The potato is an important world food crop, as it contains large amounts of carbohydrate, which provides energy. In Italy, our pasta provides the majority of our needs, but we still like the potato. All the numerous varieties available in Italy are particularly adaptable: with them we can make potato purée, potato cakes, oven-roasted potatoes, fried potatoes, potato *gnocchi*, potato soups, potato breads, and there is even a salami in Piedmont made with meat and potatoes! You can also find potato fritters, croquettes and *frittatas*, and potato alcohol (usually vodka) is often used to make the very Italian liqueur *limoncello.* A variety of sweets and savouries are made with *fécule* or potato flour. I don't know of any other vegetable that is so versatile.

The **Jerusalem artichoke** (*topinambur*) is also a tuber, and comes from North America. It has nothing to do with Jerusalem, nor is the plant related to the globe artichoke. It is a member of the sunflower family, and 'Jerusalem' is thought to be a corruption of the Italian word for sunflower, '*girasole*'. It can be eaten raw – almost exclusively in Italy to dip into a *bagna cauda* sauce – but the well-known indigestible effects (due to a substance called inulin) are greater than when it is eaten cooked. I usually use it in soups (see page 114), for purées, fried in butter or baked in the oven. It can also be cooked to serve as a filling for *ravioli* or to stuff other vegetables.

Yams and, oddly, peanuts are tubers too, but the former are not used in Italy and the latter are discussed elsewhere (see page 234).

The **sweet potato** (*patata dolce*), strictly speaking, is a tuberous root rather than a tuber, but it grows in much the same way as ordinary potatoes and Jerusalem artichokes. It is not related to the ordinary potato, and cannot grow new vegetables underground, as can potatoes (it is grown by slips or cuttings). It contains good carbohydrate and, because its flesh is dark in colour (usually red/orange), it contains beta-carotene. It is a staple food in many areas of Africa and Asia, and makes an interesting alcohol in Japan. We don't cook it much in Italy, but it is good roasted, puréed, in soups and even in some desserts. The Americans bake it in brownies and pies, and also serve it as a sweetened vegetable accompaniment to turkey at Thanksgiving.

**Celeriac** (*sedano rapa*) is the swollen stem-base or corm of an ancient type of celery. Both this root variety and the shoot variety, celery proper (see page 27), are descended from an original wild plant called smallage. The tiny roots of smallage were eaten in the sixteenth century in Europe, but by the next century the more familiar large roots had been developed. It is round, like a craggy turnip, has a sweet and intense celery flavour, and its leaves can also be eaten. It is used to make the famous French starter, *céléri rémoulade* (julienned celeriac bound with a flavoured mayonnaise), *insalata capricciosa* (which is much the same, although with more ingredients, see page 107), to make baked or fried chips, reduced to a very delicate purée together with carrot or potato, or simply baked in the oven with butter and breadcrumbs. It makes a very good soup too, a dish of the Veneto.

A final tuber in this category is the **dahlia** (*dalia*), which is best known in Europe for its stunning flowers. However, in the sixteenth century it was imported to the West more as a root vegetable, like its compatriot the potato, rather than for its floral beauty. Domesticated by the Aztecs, the tubers – known as dahlia 'yams' – were a staple food almost as important as the potatoes, avocados, tomatoes and corn that were grown alongside them. Related to Jerusalem artichokes, the tubers have a crisp apple-like texture and a flavour (depending on the variety) that varies from mild carrot or celery to asparagus and parsley. It's good in salads (coleslaw for instance), stir-fried, in stews, etc. I haven't tasted it yet, but I think I shall be doing a bit of dahlia growing...

# THE ONION FAMILY

The genus *Allium* is not large, but it is quite important and, worldwide, I don't know any cuisine or culture that doesn't use some form of onion or related vegetable. The family is the *Alliaciae*, and thus each onion-type vegetable – onion, leek, shallot, garlic, spring onions, chives – is distantly related to asparagus, lilies and tulips. The bulk of the onion grouping are bulbs, growing underground, which is why they are often called 'root' vegetables. The exception is leek, which grows above ground, but it is still an integral part of the 'family'. At one time, eating '*pane e cipolle*' was symptomatic of being poor, but not any more – the onion and all its relations are delightful accessories to good food!

The **onion** (*cipolla*) is said to have originated in Central Asia, and was taken throughout Europe by the Romans – and introduced to the Americas by Christopher Columbus! My fondest childhood memory involving onions is of my father using a slice of raw onion as a spoon, bringing some *pasta e fagioli* soup from the plate to his mouth and eating them together, the soup and the spoon! I tried to emulate this a few times, but it wasn't really to my taste!

There are many varieties of onion – large, small, strong, mild, almost too many to mention – but in general their flavour is indicated by the colour of their skin: golden onions are stronger, and are better for long cooking or where a strong onion taste is required, whereas white and red onions are milder. (The *cipolla di Tropea* is a Calabrian red onion which is so sweet in taste it can be eaten almost like an apple.) Care must be taken when preparing, as most onions contain sulphur compounds which can affect your tastebuds and your eyes when they are cut. There are many suggested solutions to the problem – often very silly – but I suggest you soak your onions in water for 30 minutes before preparing, then breathe through your mouth rather than your nose when cutting.

The onion is more of a 'foundation' vegetable than one eaten for itself. Onion forms part of a *battuto* or *soffritto*, the initial stage of most Italian dishes, soups, sauces, risottos or stews. Onion combines with almost anything and, depending on how you use it, will give a particular taste. If you sauté chopped onion gently and carefully, the natural sugars in the onion caramelize and brown, giving wonderful flavour; if burned, these sugars impart a bitter flavour. If chopped onion is sweated until transparent, without being browned, the sugars intensify, and the flavour actually becomes sweet.

Some of the traditional Italian dishes that make the best use of onion include *sardine in saor* (sweet and sour sardines) and *fegato alla veneziana* (liver with onions), both examples of Venetian cooking. The *pizzalandrea* of Genoa and the *pissaladière* of nearby

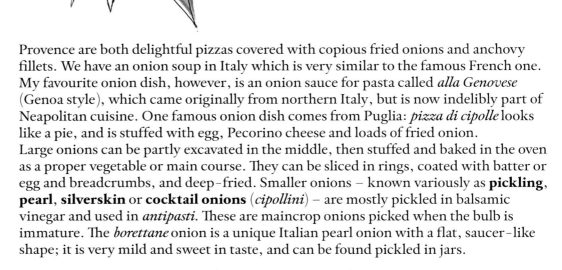

Provence are both delightful pizzas covered with copious fried onions and anchovy fillets. We have an onion soup in Italy which is very similar to the famous French one. My favourite onion dish, however, is an onion sauce for pasta called *alla Genovese* (Genoa style), which came originally from northern Italy, but is now indelibly part of Neapolitan cuisine. One famous onion dish comes from Puglia: *pizza di cipolle* looks like a pie, and is stuffed with egg, Pecorino cheese and loads of fried onion.

Large onions can be partly excavated in the middle, then stuffed and baked in the oven as a proper vegetable or main course. They can be sliced in rings, coated with batter or egg and breadcrumbs, and deep-fried. Smaller onions – known variously as **pickling**, **pearl**, **silverskin** or **cocktail onions** (*cipollini*) – are mostly pickled in balsamic vinegar and used in *antipasti*. These are maincrop onions picked when the bulb is immature. The *borettane* onion is a unique Italian pearl onion with a flat, saucer-like shape; it is very mild and sweet in taste, and can be found pickled in jars.

**Spring**, **green** or **salad onions** (*cipollotti* and *cipollini*) are also maincrop onions, but picked even earlier than pickling onions, before the bulb has formed properly; the Tropea onion mentioned on page 99 is treated similarly. They are often planted closely together, to stunt growth. These very juvenile onions are the ones to use raw, as flavourings for salads, *risottos*, *frittatas*, sandwiches. Dip them into the Tuscan *pinzimonio*, and the Piedmontese *bagna cauda* (see page 166). The smallest member of the onion family is **chives** (*erba cipollina*), which is used more as a herb (see page 228).

The **shallot** (*scalogno*) is another member of the onion genus. It grows differently, though: instead of forming a single bulb, it divides into a cluster of small bulbs or 'cloves' (rather like, but bigger than, garlic). Shallots are very French, I think, and are only used occasionally in Italy. They have a strong taste of onion, without the aggressive bite; they can be fiddly if small, so try to find 'banana' shallots, which are larger and longer. You can find very finely chopped shallots in the vinegar accompanying raw oysters, but I prefer them simply with a few drops of lemon juice. In France shallots are essential in many classic sauces such as *beurre blanc*, *béarnaise* and the *marinière* sauce base for mussels.

**Garlic**, glorious garlic or *aglio*, is very much my favourite, and is very much part of Italian cuisine, especially in the south. It is almost impossible to imagine Italian food without garlic (or tomato, but that is another story). Garlic has been known and used in cooking for thousands of years – and in medicine, for many of its natural compounds are beneficial to health. They say the Egyptian slaves who built the pyramids were given a garlic clove per day, and in Roman times garlic was used as a disinfectant for wounds, so great was its therapeutic fame.

There are basically three types of garlic, with differing coloured skins – white, pinky-red and purple. My favourite is the pink one. The bulbs vary in size, often according to the country of origin. Elephant garlic is the largest of them all. Dried garlic – the bulbs with the white papery skin – is available all year round, and fresh bulbs – which are milder in flavour, with green stalks – are found in season.

Garlic, like onion, is used more as a 'foundation' vegetable than as a vegetable in its own right, playing a part in the *battuto* and *soffritto*, the primary stages of many a sauce or stew. Its main culinary value is as a seasoning which, used judiciously, can enhance other flavours. It is wonderful in the famous garlic and anchovy dip of Piedmont, *bagna cauda* (see page 119). It is also used in the Piedmontese *soma d'ail*, bread rubbed with raw garlic and doused with olive oil: the same dish is *fettunta* in Tuscany and *bruschetta* in the south. Garlic is a primary ingredient in the Ligurian *pesto*.

But, like onion, garlic contains sulphur compounds, and these produce the famously persistent and anti-social breath odour (actually excreted in perspiration and from the lungs). There are various ways to deal with this. First, you should be aware of garlic's characteristics: the more you cut it, the more the clove's essential oils are released, and the stronger the flavour. So whole roast cloves, for instance, are mild in flavour, while finely chopped raw garlic is very pungent. Sometimes, if you need just a hint of garlic flavour, you can rub a peeled clove round the sides of the pan you are going to cook the dish in, or even around the inside of your salad bowl. You could gently fry slices of garlic in oil, and then discard the garlic: the oil will retain enough of the flavour. And if you are worried about garlicky breath, chew some raw parsley or mint, or some cardamom, anise or fennel seeds (the *paan* mixture offered after an Indian meal contains some of these seeds to freshen your breath).

I live in an area, in the south of England, where from March to May entire roadsides are covered with **wild garlic** (*aglio selvatico* or *Allium ursinum*, 'bear garlic' or ramsons). Its leaves are large (like those of lily of the valley), and when young, taste very like garlic. But it is the garlic smell, though, which is the strongest, and can alert you to the plant's presence!

You use the pretty leaves and white flowers of wild garlic, but not the bulb, which is almost non-existent. I collect the leaves in season and process them with olive oil almost like *pesto*, and freeze in ice cubes to use later in soups and sauces. I think I am responsible for introducing the catering industry to the joys of cooking with wild garlic. Very early on, at the Neal Street Restaurant and later at Carluccio's deli, I made great use of wild foods such as wild garlic, rocket and mushrooms, many of them brought to me by my friend and fellow wild-food enthusiast, Gennaro Contaldo. The only fear is that by introducing the joys of these wild foods to the general public, the wild stocks might be threatened with over-cropping. However, wild garlic can easily be cultivated: I transplanted a few plants into my London garden, and it has grown well. And rocket spreads like a weed!

My latest use of wild garlic was at Easter in 2015. With wild garlic, nettles, dandelion, wild sorrel, some rape tops, a potato and a carrot, I made a fine soup that was delicious and very seasonal.

The **leek** (*porro*) is the mildest in flavour of the onion genus, and in shape it is like an elongated onion – up to 70cm (28 inches) in length, and with layers of white at the non-globular base, and a fan of green leaves at the top. Similar to asparagus and chicory, leeks are blanched during their growth, banked up with earth to protect the bases from the light and keep them white. They need careful cleaning before use because of this.

The leek is served more as a vegetable in its own right than any other member of the onion family. Sometimes known as 'the asparagus of the poor', small leeks go well with many asparagus accompaniments such as butter, vinaigrette, cheese, eggs, ham and cream. Whole, they can be boiled, steamed, braised and grilled, and the tiniest baby leeks are delicious stir-fried. Larger specimens can be sliced and used in stocks or soups – most famously in the French leek and potato soup, *vichyssoise,* and the Scottish leek and chicken soup, cock-a-leekie. Small is best, though. In Italy, we like them with fried eggs and Parmesan in *porri alla milanese,* or braised with olive oil and tomatoes. They are used for soups, *frittate* and pasta sauces. I like them boiled and served whole as part of a winter *antipasto.* Very young leeks can be eaten raw, perhaps in the Tuscan *pinzimonio,* or with the Piedmontese *bagna cauda* (see page 166).

The final bulb I want to talk about is that of the **tassel hyacinth**, *Muscari comosum* (*lampascioni*), which is cultivated and eaten in Puglia and Basilicata. These were once a poor man's food, but now they are becoming increasingly popular. Also known as *cipolline selvatiche* (wild baby onions), they are crunchier than pickled onions, with a pungent and peppery, slightly bitter, taste. They are always cooked, sometimes pickled, never eaten raw.

# LASAGNA DI BIETOLE
*Beetroot Lasagne*

Beetroot is sold in good delicatessens in Italy already cooked. It's usually oven-baked, when the concentration of goodies is greater than with a boiled vegetable. It is better if you use large beetroots, as they will need to be cut into thin slices to build the *lasagna* layers. You could make this dish vegetarian by omitting the smoked ham.

Preheat the oven to 180°C (350°F/gas 4).

Boil the beetroot in slightly salted water for 1½ hours, until the centre is soft.

Make the sauce. Melt the butter in a medium saucepan, then add the flour, and stir to amalgamate the flour with the melted butter. Add the warm milk slowly, stirring constantly to avoid lumps, until the sauce is thick. Add 80g (2¾oz) of the Parmesan, some nutmeg, chilli powder, salt and pepper to taste.

Peel the cooked beetroot and cut into thin slices. In an ovenproof dish, build a layer of beetroot, followed by a layer of ham, then cover with some of the sauce. Build up these layers until you finish the ingredients, ending with the remainder of the sauce on top. Add a final sprinkle of the remaining Parmesan and black pepper.

Bake in the preheated oven for 35 minutes and serve hot.

SERVES 4

—4 very large beetroot (beets), about 750g (1lb 10oz)
—150g (5½oz) smoked ham, in thin slices
—salt and freshly ground black pepper

SPICY CHEESE SAUCE
—70g (2½oz) unsalted butter
—50g (1¾oz/⅓ cup) plain flour (all-purpose flour)
—500ml (18fl oz/2 cups) milk, warmed
—90g (3¼oz) Parmesan, freshly grated
—freshly grated nutmeg
—a pinch of chilli powder

## MARMELLATA DI BARBA BIETOLE
*Beetroot 'Jam'*

*Marmellata* is the word used in various European languages to denote a jam, rather than the specific usage in English, to denote a preserve made from oranges. I have made a chestnut 'jam' (see page 247), and here there is one made from sweet beetroots, perfect for breakfast or afternoon spreading: it would be perfect used as the filling for my carrot cake (see page 109).

The 'jam' could also be made with carrots. Neither of them last long, though, so use as soon as you can.

Cut the beetroots into slices, and place in a medium saucepan. Just cover with lightly salted water, add the sugar, then bring to the boil. Turn the heat down, and simmer until the liquid is syrupy and the beetroot is soft. Leave to cool.

Whiz the beetroot mixture in a blender, adding the ground cardamom.

Meanwhile, soak the gelatine leaf in a small bowl of water to soften it. Gently heat the lemon juice in a small saucepan until warm. Remove the gelatine from the water, and squeeze to get rid of the excess water. Add the softened leaf to the warm lemon juice, off the heat, and stir until melted.

Add the gelatine and juice to the beetroot mixture and process again in the blender. Put into a clean container and store in the refrigerator, for no longer than a few days.

MAKES 400G (14OZ)

—300g (10½oz) large beetroots, trimmed and lightly peeled
—salt
—100g (3½oz) golden caster sugar (superfine sugar)
—½ teaspoon ground cardamom
—1 gelatine leaf
—juice of 2 lemons

## INSALATA CAPRICCIOSA
### *Carrot, Celeriac and Artichoke Salad*

It is difficult to translate *capricciosa* into English. It suggests whimsicality or capriciousness, but in culinary terms it refers to a mixture of things (think pizza). Here it means a concoction of three raw vegetables, which, along with the help of mayonnaise, become a delight to put on bread, on pastry, in sandwiches, etc. A little portion of this *capricciosa* is usually offered as part of an *antipasto* in a similar way to Russian salad (see page 115). It is also similar to the French *céleri rémoulade*, which is served as a starter.

Once you have cut the vegetables into similar-sized pieces, put them into a large serving bowl. Mix in the mayonnaise, lemon juice and salt to taste.

This can be kept in the refrigerator for a few days.

SERVES 8–10

—200g (7oz) celeriac, peeled and cut into matchsticks
—300g (10½oz) carrots, peeled and cut into matchsticks
—250g (9oz) pickled artichokes (*carciofini*) in oil (see page 76), cut into matchsticks
—150g (5½oz) good mayonnaise (see page 115)
—juice of ½ a large lemon
—salt

# TORTA DI CAROTE
*Carrot Cake*

In Europe, during the seventeenth and eighteenth centuries, when sweeteners were expensive, carrots and parsnips were used in sweet puddings and cakes, and carrot cake has recently enjoyed a resurgence in popularity. You could also serve this as a dessert with some whipped cream: add sugar to taste and perhaps a tablespoon or so of a liqueur.

Preheat the oven to 150°C (300°F/gas 2). Use a little butter to grease a round cake tin 30cm (12 inches) in diameter.

Cut the carrots into slices, put into a medium saucepan, then cover with the orange juice. Bring to the boil, then simmer until tender. Drain, discarding the orange juice.

When cooled a little, whiz the carrots in a blender with the olive oil and egg yolks. Spoon the purée into a bowl, and fold in the sugar, sifted flour and baking powder. Separately, in a clean bowl, whisk the egg whites until stiff. Using a metal spoon, carefully fold the egg whites into the carrot mixture – you don't want to lose the air in the whites.

Pour the mixture into the prepared baking tin, and bake for 40–45 minutes. Leave to cool in the tin, then turn out of the tin on to a wire cooling rack. Leave until completely cold.

To fill, if you like, cut the cake in half horizontally, using a long, very sharp knife. Spread jam over the bottom half, and top with the top half. Chill for 30 minutes or so before serving, dusted with a little icing sugar.

MAKES 1 SPONGE, TO SERVE 10

SPONGE
—unsalted butter, for greasing
—5 medium carrots, about 1kg (2lb 4oz), trimmed and peeled
—500ml (18fl oz/2 cups) orange juice
—120ml (4fl oz/½ cup) extra virgin olive oil
—4 medium eggs, separated
—360g (12oz/1½ cups) caster sugar (superfine sugar)
—350g (12oz/2⅓ cups) Italian '00' flour, sifted
—15g (½oz) baking powder

TO FINISH AND SERVE
—a jam of choice (and see *Marmellata di Barba Bietole*, page 106)
—icing sugar (confectioners' sugar)

# PIATTO DI VEGETALI CON SALSA OLANDESE
*Bouquet of Vegetables with Hollandaise Sauce*

This starter – or it could be a main course for indestructible vegetarians – is a lovely thing to see, but especially to taste, because all the vegetables are cooked in their own time to a perfect tenderness. They offer the maximum natural flavour, underlined by a very delicate sauce.

For reasons of tenderness, and also to avoid mixing flavours, do two separate cooking sessions. Cook together the carrots, fennel and mini corn in a large saucepan of slightly salted water until slightly softened; you will have to judge this for yourself – try a piece, and see if it is *al dente* enough for you.

In another pan of lightly salted water, cook the remaining vegetables until they are to your taste, as above. Drain both pans, and keep the vegetables at room temperature.

To clarify the butter for the hollandaise, melt the butter over a very low heat, until you see a clear liquid separating from the casein or milk solids. The latter will fall to the bottom of the pan, and you should very carefully pour off the clear, or clarified, butter, leaving the solids behind.

Mix the egg yolks with the mustard and a little lemon juice in the top half of a double boiler or bain-marie (or even a bowl above, but not touching, a pan of hot water). Start to add the clarified butter gradually, as if making mayo, stirring all the time, never allowing the sauce to get too hot. It is ready when it is thick. Taste for seasoning, and add salt and pepper, or more lemon.

Arrange the vegetables on a large platter, with the bowl of hollandaise in the middle.

SERVES 4–8

—200g (7oz) baby carrots, halved if a bit larger
—2 fennel bulbs, cut into eighths
—about 150g (5½oz) mini corn
—300g (10½oz) small courgettes (zucchini), halved if a bit larger
—200g (7oz) thin asparagus spears
—200g (7oz) purple sprouting broccoli spears
—2 small *romanesco* heads, cut in half
—salt and freshly ground black pepper

HOLLANDAISE SAUCE
—400g (14oz) unsalted butter, clarified (see below)
—4–5 medium egg yolks
—1 teaspoon Dijon mustard
—juice of 1 lemon

## ZEPPOLE
*Deep-fried Potato Puffs*

It is a tradition in various Italian regions to make these deep-fried pastries, *zeppole*, at the time of the Festa di San Giuseppe or St Joseph's Day (19 March). My mother used to make quantities of these, which would promptly be devoured by us children. They can be sweet or savoury, and made of bread dough, choux pastry dough, or a *gnocchi* dough as here. They are eaten with *prosciutto* in Emilia-Romagna, where they are called *gnocco fritto*.

Should you prefer the sweet version of this recipe, omit the anchovies and fry them plainly; after draining, dust them with caster sugar (superfine sugar).

In a large bowl, mix the flour, mashed potato, yeast, salt and egg. Add just enough milk – probably about 2–4 tablespoons – to obtain a soft dough. Mix well, then cover the bowl with a damp cloth and leave in a warm place to rise for 1 hour. When the mixture has risen, it should be quite dense and thick.

In a large deep frying pan, add enough olive oil so that the pan is a third full. Place over a medium heat. To test whether the oil has reached the perfect frying temperate, drop a small piece of bread in. If it fries and goes golden, the oil is ready.

Take a tablespoonful of mixture, push an anchovy into the centre and enclose it to create a container. Fry in the hot oil until golden on both sides. Drain on absorbent kitchen paper, while you cook the remaining mixture and the rest of the anchovies. Serve the fritters immediately as they are made.

SERVES 6–8, ABOUT 40 FRITTERS

—700g (1lb 9oz/5¼ cups) Italian '00' flour
—450g (1lb) potatoes, boiled until tender, peeled and mashed
—15g (½oz) fresh yeast, dissolved in water (or the equivalent dried yeast)
—10g (¼oz) salt
—1 medium egg, beaten
—milk as required, to obtain a soft dough
—olive oil, for deep-frying
—at least 2 x 50g (1¾oz) tins of anchovy fillets in oil, drained

# PURE DI PATATE TARTUFATE
## *Truffled Potato Purée*

A simple but excellent combination of flavours, this mashed potato can accompany many dishes as a side dish. It is especially good with the venison on page 269.

Boil the potatoes in plenty of slightly salted water with a little saffron until very soft. Drain well and reduce to a purée with the milk. Add the butter, Parmesan, salt and pepper to taste, and the truffle oil. Should you also have the truffle, cut it into thick slices, then into small cubes. Mix these into the potato purée, or sprinkle on top.

SERVES 4

— 600g (1lb 5oz) floury potatoes, peeled and cubed
— a little pinch of saffron strands
— 6 tablespoons milk
— 30g (1oz) unsalted butter
— 20g (¾oz) Parmesan, freshly grated
— 2 teaspoons truffle oil
— 20g (¾oz) black truffle (optional)
— salt and freshly ground black pepper

*other roots*

113

# TORTA RUSTICA DI PATATE
## *Rustic Potato Cake*

When we were children, if we had this rustic potato cake for lunch or dinner, we knew the larder or refrigerator had been thoroughly raided. A piece of salami or ham here, a piece of cheese for flavour there, eggs, parsley, salt and pepper. We were always quite happy about my mother's choice. She was best at producing the cake; we were best at eating it!

Preheat the oven to 180°C (350°F/gas 4).

Boil the potatoes in salted water until tender, then drain and peel them. Pass them through a potato ricer (or sieve) to make a purée. Mix the potato purée with the ham, mozzarella, Provola, Parmesan, beaten eggs, parsley and some salt and pepper.

Use the butter to grease a round cake tin 25cm (10 inches) in diameter, and dust with some of the breadcrumbs. Spoon the potato mixture into this, and press gently with a fork to give some shape. Sprinkle with the remaining breadcrumbs, then trickle over the olive oil.

Bake in the preheated oven for 35–40 minutes, until browned on top. Serve in slices. The cake is very good warm, but also excellent cold.

SERVES 6

- 1kg (2lb 4oz) floury potatoes
- 55g (2oz) cooked ham, cut into cubes
- 25g (1oz) buffalo mozzarella cheese, cut into small cubes
- 150g (5½oz) Provola cheese (smoked mozzarella), cut into small cubes
- 55g (2oz) Parmesan, freshly grated
- 4 medium eggs, beaten
- 2 tablespoons finely chopped fresh flat-leaf parsley
- a knob of unsalted butter
- 4 tablespoons dried white breadcrumbs
- 4 tablespoons extra virgin olive oil
- salt and freshly ground black pepper

# ZUPPA DI TOPINAMBOUR, PORRO E PROSCIUTTO DI PARMA
## *Jerusalem Artichoke and Leek Soup with Parma Ham*

The usual way of using Jerusalem artichokes in Italy is raw, with the dip *bagna cauda*, although it is also wonderful braised. Many European cuisines have a soup made from this vegetable, and this is my take on it, with the addition of the delicacy of some leek, and the savouriness of the Parmesan. This combination makes for a truly warm-hearted soup.

Serve with croûtons if you like. Toast a couple of slices of good country bread until golden, then rub with garlic (as for *bruschetta*). Cut into cubes, and fry in butter as outlined below.

Prepare all the vegetables first. Cut the artichokes into chunks. Trim the leeks of roots and tough leaves, then cut into chunks.

Heat the olive oil in a large saucepan and sauté the artichokes and leeks. After 10 minutes, add the stock, cover and cook for about 25 minutes. The artichokes should be soft and starting to turn into a purée, and the leeks will be tender.

Separately, in a frying pan, melt the butter and fry the Parma ham and the croûtons (if using) until crisp. Drain on absorbent kitchen paper. Serve the ham and croûtons on top of the soup, then sprinkle each helping with Parmesan.

SERVES 4–6

—400g (14oz) Jerusalem artichokes, peeled weight
—2 leeks, 100g (3½oz) each
—2 tablespoons extra virgin olive oil
—1.5 litres (2¾ pints / 6 cups) vegetable stock

TO SERVE
—25g (1oz) unsalted butter
—50g (1¾oz) Parma ham, cut into very fine cubes
—50g (1¾oz) croûtons (optional)
—20g (¾oz) Parmesan, freshly grated

## INSALATA RUSSA
### Russian Salad

This salad, consisting of cooked vegetables served in a coating of mayonnaise, is a salad enjoyed by almost every Piedmontese, as it is always included in *antipasto*. It gained its name because the recipe, or something very like it, became famous in Moscow in the nineteenth century. Three influential French chefs opened a noted restaurant, and one of them, M. Olivier, is said to have invented this. Indeed, in many countries, the salad is known as Olivier salad. How it reached Piedmont, I do not know…

Make the mayonnaise first. Preferably using a hand-held whisk, in a bowl, beat the yolks with the mustard and a pinch each of salt and pepper until the mixture becomes creamy. Stirring continuously, add a little stream of the olive oil. Beat again until this has amalgamated. Continue adding a little oil at a time, beating all the while, until the mixture has become fluffy and has increased in volume, and all the oil has been beaten in. Now add the lemon juice and mix well. Cover the bowl with clingfilm (plastic wrap) until needed.

Cook all the vegetables for the salad in slightly salted water until al dente. You don't want them *too* soft. Drain well, and leave to cool down.

When cold, mix the vegetables carefully with the tuna, vinegar and some salt and pepper to taste. Fold them gently into the mayonnaise until the mixture binds together. Store in the refrigerator.

SERVES 6

—250g (9oz) small new potatoes, scrubbed and finely diced
—250g (9oz) carrots, peeled and finely diced
—200g (7oz) celeriac, peeled and finely diced
—150g (5¹⁄₂oz) small turnips, peeled and finely diced
—100g (3¹⁄₂oz) each of small cauliflower and calabrese broccoli florets
—200g (7oz) broad beans (fava beans) (frozen are fine)
—150g (5¹⁄₂oz) good tinned tuna in oil, drained and finely flaked
—1 tablespoon white wine vinegar

MAYONNAISE
—3 medium egg yolks
—1 teaspoon English or Dijon mustard, to taste
—salt and freshly ground black pepper
—250ml (9fl oz/1 cup) light olive oil
—juice of ¹⁄₂ a lemon

# SOMA, FETTUNTA, BRUSCHETTA
*Bread with Oil and Garlic*

They call it *soma d'ail* in Piedmont, *fettunta* in Tuscany and *bruschetta* in the south of Italy, but basically it is the same: a slice of good *ciabatta* or country bread, toasted or preferably 'grilled', with a garlic clove gently rubbed on it, then doused with excellent extra virgin olive oil. It is eaten by itself or to accompany *antipasto*, and can be covered with a topping, such as chopped tomato and basil.

—2 garlic cloves, peeled
—8 slices of very good bread, toasted or grilled
—a little stream of extra virgin olive oil
—salt and freshly ground black pepper

Extremely simple. Rub the garlic cloves gently over the surface of the toasted bread, pressing more or less, depending on your taste. Pour a little olive oil on the top.

Season with salt and pepper and *buon appetito!*

SERVES 4

*onion family*

# AGLIATA
## *Garlic and Hazelnut Paste*

As the French have *aïoli,* which is mayonnaise with garlic paste in it, so the Italians have *agliata.* This paste is more unusual, however, preserving two of the most coveted items in Piedmont, garlic and hazelnuts. It can be used in different ways. Spread it on *crostini* for a snack, add it to the stuffing of a roast for flavour, or use it as a sauce for spaghetti: cook 250g (9oz) of spaghetti as normal in salted water and add a couple of tablespoons of *agliata* to the pasta when drained, along with 2 tablespoons of the cooking water to let it down to a sauce-like texture.

Prepare the garlic, hazelnuts and parsley. Cut the crusts off the bread, then crumble the bread to crumbs. Mix everything together in a bowl, until paste-like. Add some salt and pepper to taste.

Store the paste in the refrigerator for a couple of days if not using straight away.

SERVES 4–5

—20g (¾oz) garlic cloves, peeled and reduced to a paste
—20g (¾oz) shelled hazelnuts, toasted and finely chopped
—15g (½oz) roughly chopped fresh flat-leaf parsley
—1 slice of white bread
—20g (¾oz) Parmesan, freshly grated
—50ml (2fl oz/¼ cup) extra virgin olive oil
—salt and freshly ground black pepper

# FRITTATA DI PORRI E GAMBERETTI
*Omelette of Leeks and Prawn*

Leeks have a flavour of their own, between onion and shallot. They are very good in combination with prawns (shrimp), in fact I could even envisage them with scallops. I usually cook a *frittata* with olive oil rather than butter, as I like it eaten cold as well as hot. The oil does not congeal, as the butter would.

Another suggestion is to cook very small leeks like you would asparagus, and serve them with vinaigrette. This is a very nice starter.

- 300g (10½oz) small–medium leeks, well trimmed and washed
- 150g (5½oz) shelled prawns (shrimp)
- extra virgin olive oil
- 10 medium eggs
- 60g (2¼oz) Parmesan, freshly grated
- salt and freshly ground black pepper

Cut the leeks into little chunks. Shell the prawns.

Heat 2 tablespoons of the olive oil in a 25cm (10 inch) frying pan and fry the leeks gently until soft, about 10 minutes. Add the prawns and cook for another 5 minutes until the prawns turn pink.

Beat the eggs in a large bowl, and stir in the Parmesan and some salt and pepper to taste.

Heat a little more oil in the frying pan, then add the egg mixture to the leeks and prawns. Cook gently, to let it solidify on one side, about 10 minutes. Every now and again use a spatula to gently loosen the bottom of the omelette from the sides, which allows some of the liquid mixture to hit the base of the pan and set. When there is no more liquid left, put a plate over the top of the pan and invert the omelette on to the plate, then slide it back into the pan, uncooked side down. Add the remaining oil, and brown the other side, about 5–6 minutes.

Serve hot or cold.

SERVES 4–6

*onion family*

# ZUPPA DI PANE E AGLIO
*Bread and Garlic Soup*

A hearty soup such as this exists in some form or another in many countries across the world. It is a combination of simple, but flavourful, ingredients, and could be seen as a symbol of *la cucina povera*, poor but delicious food. In my opinion, a soup like this is one of the simplest but tastiest ways to enjoy minimalism.

Put the stock, sliced garlic and sliced potatoes into a large saucepan and bring to the boil. Turn the heat down and simmer for 30 minutes, or until both the potatoes and garlic are soft. Process in a blender until broken down and smooth, then add salt and pepper to taste.

Toast the slices of bread – or grill them. Cut the whole garlic clove in half and rub gently on the bread. Drizzle with a little olive oil.

Pour the soup into four bowls. Add the slices of bread on top of the soup, sprinkled with the cheese, and serve.

SERVES 4

—1.5 litres (2³/₄ pints / 6 cups) vegetable or chicken stock
—100g (3¹/₂oz) garlic cloves, peeled and finely sliced
—300g (10¹/₂oz) floury potatoes, peeled and sliced
—salt and freshly ground black pepper

TO SERVE
—4 slices of *ciabatta* bread
—1 garlic clove, peeled and left whole
—extra virgin olive oil
—2 tablespoons freshly grated Parmesan

# CIPOLLINE IN AGRODOLCE
## *Sweet and Sour Pickled Onions*

One of the most desirable elements of an *antipasto* spread is sweet and sour onions. For this the best is the *borettane* onion, a small flat onion the size of a plum, which is grown all over Italy. Using balsamic vinegar to pickle these onions makes them irresistible, but beware, they are not pickled enough to enable you to keep them for a long time.

Heat the olive oil in a large saucepan and fry the onions gently until soft, about 10 minutes. Add the vinegar, sugar, salt and a few grates of nutmeg, and continue to fry very gently for 15 minutes.

Eat straight away, or put into a clean jar and keep in the refrigerator for a few days only.

FILLS I X 500G (18OZ) JAR

—2 tablespoons extra virgin olive oil
—500g (1lb 2oz) *borettane* onions, or small pickling or pearl onions, peeled and cleaned
—6 tablespoons balsamic vinegar
—50g (1³⁄₄oz / ¹⁄₄ cup) caster sugar (superfine sugar)
—15g (¹⁄₂oz) salt
—freshly grated nutmeg

# PIZZA ALL' ANDREA (PISSALADIÈRE)
*Pizza with Onions and Anchovies*

The French and Italian Riviera share this delightful breakfast or quick snack that you can buy from bakeries or delicatessens. It is usually produced in large, oblong trays of which you buy a square, but you can also make it as a round pizza.

Dissolve the fresh yeast in the warm water to which you have added the salt and olive oil. Pour the flour into a mound on a clean surface and make a well in the centre. Add the yeast mixture drop by drop into the well in the flour, mixing by hand until all the liquid is absorbed, forming large lumps. Knead the dough with your hands until it has a smooth texture, then roll it into a ball. A good pizza depends on the quality of the dough used. (If using dried yeast, simply add this to the flour before mixing in the liquids.)

Next, sprinkle some flour into a large bowl and place the dough in it. Spread a little extra olive oil over the top to prevent a crust from forming. Cover the bowl with a dry cloth and leave to rise for an hour in a warm place, no less than 20°C (70°F). (It was at this stage that my grandmother used to 'bless the dough' by making the sign of the cross in order that it should turn out well.) After this time the volume of the dough should have increased threefold.

Now begins the preparation of the pizza proper. Preheat the oven to 230°C (450°F/gas 8). Grease four 27cm (10¾ inch) pizza tins with olive oil. Flour the working surface.

CONTINUED OVERLEAF...

## BASIC PIZZA DOUGH
### (MAKES 4 X 27CM ROUND PIZZAS)
—25g (1oz) fresh yeast (or the equivalent dried yeast: see maker's instructions)
—150ml (5fl oz/⅔ cup) warm water
—a pinch of salt
—2 tablespoons extra virgin olive oil
—400g (14oz/2½ cups) plain flour (all-purpose flour)

## TOPPING
—500g (1lb 2oz) white onions, peeled and finely sliced
—extra virgin olive oil
—20 anchovy fillets in oil

*onion family*

**125**

## PIZZA ALL' ANDREA (PISSALADIÈRE)
*Pizza with Onions and Anchovies*

Divide the dough into four and shape each piece into a ball. Flatten the dough out using a rolling pin. Starting from the middle, smooth the dough out to a thickness of about 6mm (¼ inch). I suggest you make the edges slightly thicker to prevent the topping from running off, and this method of rolling leaves the characteristic round edge which should go crisp in the oven.

Meanwhile, you will have been cooking the white onions in 2–3 tablespoons of olive oil in a large frying pan. Fry gently until the onions are soft and slightly coloured, about 10 minutes.

Place each pizza on the oiled pizza tins, and spread with the onions. Arrange the anchovies across the top in a lattice pattern. Bake in the preheated oven for between 8 and 15 minutes.

SERVES 4

PIZZA ALL' ANDREA
(PISSALADIÈRE)
*Pizza with Onions and Anchovies*
*Pages 125–6*

# BIGOLI IN SALSA GENOVESE
*Pasta with Onion and Tomato Sauce*

*Bigoli* is a Venetian pasta, hand-made, which resembles very large spaghetti. As it can't be found all that easily, I suggest using *bucatini* instead, which are spaghetti with a hole in the centre. The title is indeed confusing, because although the *bigoli* are Venetian and the sauce is called Genovese, from Genoa, the dish is now most associated with Naples. Clear?

First make the sauce. Heat the olive oil in a large saucepan and fry the onions gently until soft, about 10 minutes. Add the tomatoes and cook gently for 30 minutes, stirring occasionally.

Cook the pasta in boiling salted water until *al dente*, about 10 minutes. Drain well.

Add the beaten eggs to the tomato sauce, and stir quickly to thicken the sauce. Season with salt and pepper to taste. Mix the sauce with the pasta and top with the grated Parmesan.

SERVES 4

—350g (12oz) *bucatini* pasta
—50g (1³/₄oz) Parmesan, freshly grated
—salt and freshly ground black pepper

SAUCE
—4 tablespoons extra virgin olive oil
—200g (7oz) onions, peeled and sliced
—1 x 400g (14oz) tin of chopped tomatoes
—2 large eggs, beaten

# CIPOLLE RIPIENE
*Stuffed Onions*

The Italians like to stuff any type of vegetable that lends itself to this purpose. Courgettes (zucchini), aubergines (eggplants), artichokes, tomatoes, bell peppers, olives and courgette flowers can, with some differences, be stuffed with the following mixture. If you are vegetarian, avoid the meat used in the filling below, and look through this book for other non-meat fillings – there are quite a few.

Peel the onions. Cook them in a large saucepan of lightly salted water for 10 minutes. Drain. When cool enough to handle, cut the tops off the onions and scoop out the centre two-thirds of the pulp. Keep this, and finely chop it for the stuffing. You will be left with an onion shell, with the outer layers intact.

Heat the olive oil in a large frying pan, and fry the crumbled meat of the sausage together with the chopped onion for about 10 minutes to cook the meat. Leave to cool down.

Preheat the oven to 180°C (350°F/gas 4).

Add the remaining ingredients to the meat mixture, and season with salt and pepper to taste. Mix well and use the mixture to stuff the onions.

Place the stuffed onions on a baking tray, sprinkle with a little olive oil and bake in the preheated oven for 20–25 minutes. They can be eaten hot or cold.

SERVES 4

—8 red or white onions, the size of small oranges

STUFFING
—1 tablespoon extra virgin olive oil, plus extra for sprinkling
—200g (7oz) *lucanica* sausage, meat removed from the skin
—the insides of the boiled onions
—1 tablespoon soft raisins
—1 tablespoon pine nuts
—freshly grated nutmeg
—a pinch of ground cinnamon
—3 tablespoons fresh breadcrumbs
—1 amaretti biscuit, crumbled
—1 tablespoon freshly grated Parmesan
—1 medium egg, beaten
—salt and freshly ground black pepper

*onion family*

# VEGETABLE FRUITS

The vegetables I have written about so far come from various parts of different plants. Celery, for instance, is a classic stem vegetable; cabbage and lettuce are leaf vegetables; cauliflower and broccoli are bud vegetables; and carrots, onions and potatoes are all included in the (somewhat arbitrary) category of root vegetables. However, fruit vegetables, or vegetable fruits, are actually the *fruits* of their parent plant. They grow on vines, developing from a flower; their bodies are pulpy and contain single or many seeds, from which the next generation of plants might develop. Botanically, they are classified as fruit – primarily because of that seed content – although most of them are known and treated as vegetables.

One plant family with many vegetable fruits is the *Cucurbitaceae*, which originated in Central and South America. Members include the melons and watermelon; most of the pumpkins and squashes (known as winter squashes); the cucumber and gherkin; and the vegetable marrow and courgettes or zucchini (known as summer squashes).

Other vegetable fruits, also hailing from the Americas, are the bush fruits such as tomatoes, peppers and chillies, as well as aubergines (eggplants), the latter from Asia. Tree fruits are avocado and olive, both of which have an interior seed/stone – like a plum, for instance – but which are categorized as vegetables. Strictly speaking, in a botanical sense, peas and beans are vegetable fruits too, as the 'fruits', the pods, contain seeds.

## WINTER SQUASHES

Winter squashes belong to the genus *Cucurbita maxima*. These are the ones that can be stored through the winter; they have skins which thicken and harden, and thus protect the flesh during storage; their seeds too are fully formed. Belonging to the genus *C. pepo*, summer squashes, on the whole, are harvested when immature, with soft skin and barely visible seeds – but there are types of squash which can be considered as either. Some so-called winter squashes can be picked early and cooked without peeling, but most are grown on and stored, when the skin becomes hard and the flesh more fibrous.

Late summer and autumn is the time when winter squashes such as **pumpkin** (*zucca*) are available, as well as a plethora of other squashes and gourds (many of the latter used as decoration). We all know that pumpkins came from America: the pumpkin plays a major part in Thanksgiving celebrations, candied as a vegetable to accompany turkey, or as a gloriously sweet and spiced pumpkin pie. We adopted it enthusiastically in Italy, and pumpkin to me means those large bright orange wedges to be baked and used as a stuffing for *ravioli di zucca*, a speciality of Cremona in Lombardy. It is also pulped for use in soups and risottos, or pickled – I have developed a sweet and sour pumpkin dish that I use as an *antipasto* or as a side dish for a roast (see page 148). In Britain pumpkin is now the vegetable of choice to be carved out at Hallowe'en (it was once the swede, a rather more difficult task). And you must never waste the seeds of pumpkin. They are not just for the birds, but can be eaten after drying and roasting: scatter over breakfast fruit or into a salad, or just eat in the hand, as they do in Near Eastern and Middle Eastern countries, sold at small stands by the roadside. And, in Austria, there is a wonderful dark and flavourful oil made from pumpkin seeds; it's used mostly in Austrian cooking, but has the depth of sesame oil (almost) and should be better known.

Other winter squashes include the butternut, kabocha, Marina di Chioggia and acorn. The **butternut squash**, shaped like a medieval musical instrument – wide at the foot, thinner at the top – has a sweet intense flavour similar to pumpkin, and, like all the squashes, can be baked, stuffed, grilled, used in soups, breads, pies, risottos, etc. The **kabocha squash** is known in Australia and New Zealand as the Japanese pumpkin (it was developed in the East). **Marina** or **Piena di Chioggia** comes from the Veneto, obviously, and it is an amazing squash, shaped like a turban, with a warty skin worthy of the wartiest toad. It is known locally as *suca baruca* (warty pumpkin) and was once a baked treat offered by street-vendors. The **acorn squash,** although belonging to the summer squash genus, is used as a winter squash.

The most curious of winter squashes is, however, the **spaghetti squash**. Although a *C. pepo*, it is classified as a winter squash. When raw, the flesh inside the squash is solid and very similar to other squashes; but when cooked the flesh between seeds and skin turns to strands which resemble, and can be used as, spaghetti. And then there is the **cucuzza squash** from the south of Italy, which is also known as super-long squash or snake squash (and as *zucca lunga* or *zucchino rampicante*). It can grow up to 1.5 metres (5 feet) in length. It is easy to grow, is delicious to eat, and can be used as either a summer or winter squash. In Sicily this type of squash is candied for use in the local speciality dessert, *cassata siciliana*.

Squash and pumpkin flowers – try to use the male ones, which will not form fruit – can be used as we use courgette (zucchini) flowers. They are smaller than courgette flowers, but have a more intense flavour.

# SUMMER SQUASHES

Summer squashes belong to the same family as winter squashes, being Cucurbits, and are classified botanically as *C. pepo*, with various subspecies. On the whole, the following summer squashes are harvested when immature, and most cannot develop skins thick enough to protect them during storage. Their seeds are immature as well. None of them should ever be over-cooked, as the flesh reduces to a mush.

The best-known summer squash, certainly in Italy, is the **zucchino** ('little pumpkin'). This is the Italian name, which has been also adopted in America; it is the French name, **courgette** ('little squash'), by which it is known in the UK. *Zucchini* have long been appreciated on the Continent, but it was only in the 1950s and 1960s, primarily through the writings of Elizabeth David, that they were introduced to the UK.

The courgette produces a fruit and a pretty flower, both widely used in Italian cooking. It is a plant grown all over the world and is very prolific, producing fruits all through the summer and even in autumn, at the end of its life, in my London garden. It gives me great pleasure to use the last fruits and their tops for a delicious soup. In fact in the south of Italy a variety of courgette is grown especially for its tender shoots (often the *zucca lunga* mentioned on page 137), which are sold as *tenerume*, used in a soupy *minestra*. Courgettes can be sliced, fried in oil and marinated with garlic and mint to make *scapece*, or cut into longish slices to be either grilled or fried in batter, and can even be baked for a *parmigiana*, with cheese (like aubergine, see page 156). When young and tender, courgettes can be eaten raw, as crudités with *bagna cauda* (see page 166) for instance. At one point, courgettes needed to be salted (like aubergines) to draw out some of the water from the flesh. This is not so necessary now.

Courgettes come in a wide range of sizes and shapes, from the familiar oval green, to bright yellow and striped balloons. If you let them grow on, they produce the vegetable marrow, which is popular in England, but nowhere else to my knowledge. This can be stuffed and baked. Like other plants in the squash family, courgettes have edible flowers. The non-fruit-bearing male flowers, grown on a thin stem, are sold in bunches in Italian markets; the female flowers, often still attached to their courgette fruit, are rarer. Both flowers can be stuffed with ricotta and other flavours, or battered, and deep-fried, and there is a delicious courgette flower risotto. (Do investigate the interior of the flowers first: they could be a home for insect life!)

Another typical summer squash is the **cucumber** (*cetriolo*). Many members of the Cucurbit family originate from the Americas, but cucumbers are thought to come from South India, and to be one of the oldest cultivated vegetables (over 3,000 years). There are many varieties – among them the long British, the stubby American and the prickly Asian – but all are similar in flavour and texture. Like many of their relatives, they contain a huge amount of water, some 96 per cent, so they are the mildest tasting of all – but also the most refreshing, perhaps their principal culinary quality. As a result they are mostly used raw in salads, and the British seem to have a thing about thinly sliced cucumber in sandwiches. Cucumbers are good diced in yoghurt for the Indian *raita* and the Greek *tzatziki*, they make crunchy crudités for dips, and slices to decorate poached salmon. In my Neal Street restaurant I used to produce a cold summer soup based on puréed cucumber and tomato (see page 153). Cucumbers can also be cooked, a good accompaniment for fish or chicken, and pickled, especially the very small variety called **gherkins** (*cetriolini* in Italian, *cornichons* in French). Of the pickled cucumbers, I like the medium-sized ones, flavoured with vinegar, sugar, dill and coriander seeds, which goes fantastically well with cold meats or roast pork. The Americans like cucumbers and gherkins with dill, thus the American 'dill pickles'.

# BUSH AND TREE FRUITS

From the fruit of trees and bushes, at least a third of all Italian food can be produced, either by itself, or combined with other ingredients. Much of popular Italian cooking, especially that of the south, is based on using bush and tree fruits in imaginative ways to produce tasty and substantial dishes. These were able to substitute for expensive meat and fish, making food that was affordable for everybody, including the very poorest. The recipes would have been developed over centuries by the farmers and *contadini* (peasants), eating what they could grow and produce. I myself often prefer to eat a well prepared and flavoured, not too elaborate, dish of vegetables, quite without meat. It is enough for me to eat something like a *parmigiana* of aubergine or *zucchini*, or both together, to understand the significance of such a philosophy.

Most of the bush fruits I talk about here come originally from the Americas. Peppers – both sweet and chilli – and tomatoes come from the same family, the *Solanaceae*, as do the potato, tobacco and, rather more alarmingly, deadly nightshade. The aubergine belongs to this family as well, but its origins, for some reason, are thought to be Asian, possibly brought to Spain by the Moors. All of them were regarded, post the Columbian Exchange (see page 22), with great suspicion in Europe, with the fruits being ignored and the plants grown for decoration. In France, the ladies of the court used to wear potato flowers (which are rather pretty) in their hair! Aubergines, for instance, were thought to cause epilepsy, and this is reflected in the Italian and Greek names, *melanzana* and *melitzana* (which both mean 'apple of madness').

That aforesaid **aubergine** (*melanzana*) is a fruit that comes in a variety of shapes and colours. Some of the first seen in Europe may have been white and round (thus the alternative name of 'eggplant', used particularly in America), but most of the ones we see are dark violet in colour, shaped like a fat policeman's truncheon. Other types are pea aubergines (small, green, used in Asian curries) and green aubergines, which are very long and thin, like fat runner beans. They all grow on low bushy plants, with prickly stems and leaves (the calyx can 'sting' you). They have a yellow–green flesh, which is full of seeds if the fruit is quite mature.

Aubergines, like their cousin, the potato, must be cooked. Aubergine flesh used to be bitter and so once needed to be 'degorged' with salt, but this bitterness has now been bred out. It is still a good idea to salt, though, as this breaks down the cells of the flesh slightly, helping prevent those same cells absorbing cooking oil. (To avoid aubergine soaking up oil, you could blanch pieces instead in boiling water.) Aubergine can be fried – the best way is *al funghetto* – or stewed as part of a Sicilian speciality, *caponata* (the Italian equivalent of the French *ratatouille*), and a wonderful pasta sauce. Slices can be grilled, fried plain or coated in egg and flour for a *parmigiana*. It can be pickled from raw with vinegar, garlic, oregano and garlic for an excellent antipasto. Medallions can be baked in the oven. When boiled and squeezed dry, aubergine flesh can be mixed with minced meat (ground meat) and flavours to make wonderful patties or fritters. Aubergine can be stuffed either by hollowing out the pulp and replacing it with a flavoursome filling, or cooked in slices and rolled with a filling inside.

The **sweet pepper** or capsicum (*peperone*) is another very versatile vegetable, imported originally from the Americas, which became naturalized in Europe, especially in Italy. (I find it very interesting that it was only at this time, when peppers were introduced, that many national cuisines gained their defining culinary characteristic: India its chillies, Hungary its paprika – a spice made from peppers – and the Mediterranean its sweet peppers.)

Sweet peppers can be eaten raw or cooked. There are many types and they come in many colours – green, red, yellow, even black and orange. Some are almost square in shape, quite fleshy, and some are shaped like a horn, the flesh of which is thinner, but all have seeds inside (even in sweet peppers, these can be hot). Peppers can be grilled, roasted and eaten as salad, fried, pickled sweet-sour and stuffed. When I was a child we had a big *damigiana*, a large glass container with wickerwork around it and a big aperture at the top. In this my mother used to preserve fleshy peppers called *pepacelle* in pure white wine vinegar. The taste of those peppers when cooked together with pork was delightful, and it was mostly me who was in charge of fishing the peppers out of their liquid. Yes, peppers were then also cooked whole, especially a small green variety called *friarielli*, fried in oil and eaten with the seeds. Today a Spanish variety called *pimientos de Padrón*, from Galicia, is quite fashionable, and eaten in the same way. A special category, but no less important, are very small red peppers, the size of a walnut, which are slightly hot in flavour: these can be deseeded and stuffed either with a flavoured cheese or with a mixture of thyme and breadcrumbs. You find these as an *antipasto* or finger food.

And I cannot forget the essential **chillies** (*peperoncini*) that are used mostly in more southerly Italian regions such as Abruzzo, Puglia, Calabria, Sicily, Campania and Sardinia. There you can often see chillies hanging in long strings from balconies and windows, ready to be used in a myriad sauces, salamis, sausages and stews. They are closely related to sweet peppers, but the seeds, white membrane and skin all have much more of the alkaloid capsaicin, which is pungent to hot in effect. *Spaghetti aglio, olio e peperoncino* (spaghetti with garlic, oil and chilli) is reputedly an aphrodisiac. It's probably the simplest of Italian recipes, often eaten as a midnight feast, when one comes home late, still a bit peckish. The chilli – or *diavoletti/diavolilli* as they are called in dialect – is a much desired flavouring but only in certain Italian dishes, one of which of course is the *all'arrabbiata* (angry) sauce for pasta. As well as using chillies in very spicy sausages, along with fennel seeds, Calabria has two further chilli specialities. One is called *'nduja*, a paste based on pork fat and chilli, and the other *rosamarine*, a mixture of chilli with newly hatched fish (*neonata*). My mother was a champion at producing an offal stew made of lung, heart and liver of either pig or lamb, along with a load of chillies. Called *soffritto di maiale*, it is eaten in winter to warm up the stomach and, in my opinion, the brain as well (see page 177)! Chilli peppers are also dried in Italy to make chilli powder (*peperoncino inpoldere*) and cayenne pepper (*pepe di cayenna*).

The **avocado** (*avocado*) is a relatively new fruit in Italy. Trees have been planted in the south – they are originally from the Americas – but the fruit is mostly imported as yet. Avocados are usually eaten raw, although they can be cooked, very briefly. Their skin is inedible. The avocado has the highest protein and fat content of any fruit – over 20 per cent of its weight is fat (which is mostly good, monounsaturated and polyunsaturated). When cutting an avocado, immediately rub the cut surfaces with lemon or lime juice, or the flesh will discolour.

The most useful role of avocado is as an appetizer, halved, the large stone removed, and stuffed with prawns and mayonnaise, vinaigrette or a crab salad. They can also be used in salads – in Italy for the *insalata tricolore* (along with tomatoes and mozzarella), or to make a spread or dip (the most famous being the Mexican *guacamole*).

And where would Italian food be without **olives** (*olive*)? Olive trees are native to the Mediterranean, and have been grown in Italy for at least 2,000 years. Each of the eighteen regions produces olives – both for eating, and for oil – often growing the trees in fairly difficult conditions (for most of Italy is mountainous!). For instance, in Liguria (which produces a delicious oil), the trees are grown on steep terraces that can only be reached on foot, and of course the olives have therefore to be picked by hand. Olive oil is a staple ingredient of the Italian kitchen, produced by pressing various types of olives at various stages of ripeness. The best is obviously extra virgin olive oil, which is preferably produced from newly hand-picked olives, which are then cold-pressed for their wonderful oil. This is perfect in salads and dressings. Lesser oils can be used for cooking.

The olive fruits themselves, if to be eaten in the hand rather than made into oil, have to be treated before use as they are very bitter. They are cured for some time in water and brine, and then preserved. Thereafter they can be oven-baked, semi-dried and flavoured with the likes of garlic, chilli, fennel, or stuffed (with anchovies or slivered almonds). They can be eaten with bread as an *antipasto* – they're good as an accompaniment to a glass of wine – and they can be stuffed and fried as they do in Ascoli (see page 178) in the Marche region.

The **tomato** (*pomodoro*) is probably the most important vegetable fruit in Italy, forming the backbone of much of Italian cooking, although, again, it has only been known in Italy since around the sixteenth century, after the Columbian Exchange (see page 22). The Italian word '*pomodoro*' means 'golden fruit', as the first tomatoes introduced were yellow. Tomatoes are so valued now because they can be used fresh, or tinned or preserved in some way. I could not cook without them.

The latest news about tomatoes is the development of one weighing more than a kilogram (a couple of pounds). I wouldn't know how to deal with that (perhaps throw it, at politicians or villains?), as I am very happy with the *cuore di bue* (oxheart), the biggest available so far. I quite like the *pomodorini* of Puglia, a cherry-sized tomato, which can be kept all winter, hanging like bunches of grapes and used mostly to make fresh sauces. They shrink and are quite tough, which is why they can be preserved for a long time, but are extremely sweet in taste. Tomatoes for salads, especially in the north of Italy, are eaten almost green; they are also good when they start to blush, but I prefer ripe and red like those which produce the best tomato sauces. My granny used to preserve tomatoes in two ways. She would pulp them, let them dry slowly in the sun, then use them as a concentrated tomato paste. She would also use the elongated plum variety looking like a little flask (San Marzano type), cut into quarters (*filetti*), put them into a bottle with a large opening, like a milk bottle, with salt and some basil, and sterilize them. Even though the industry offers such a great variety of preserved tomatoes in tins, jars and tubes, many people in Italy are still nostalgic for the old days, and produce the occasional '*pomodoro in bottiglia*'.

To sterilize bottles and jars, wash them thoroughly and dry in a hot oven at 220°C (425°F/gas 7) for 30 minutes, allow to cool before filling but do not allow anything to touch the insides.

Tomatoes can be eaten raw in various salads, or used as the topping of a *bruschetta*: they can be part of a *pommarola*, a Neapolitan sauce for pasta, a chutney or, after getting rid of the seeds and membrane, fresh tomatoes can be stuffed with rice, tuna or breadcrumbs and baked. From sun-dried to sun-blushed to preserved in their own juice, the tomato is omnipresent in any Italian larder and in most Italian meals... I am writing only five basic recipes here for you, but tomato recipes in Italy are endless.

# RISOTTO CON ZUCCA
## *Pumpkin / Squash Risotto*

Pumpkin can be used in pasta dishes, in soups and, in this case, in a risotto. This is a very simple recipe, much loved in Lombardy and throughout the Po Valley – where, of course, most of the Italian risotto rice is grown. You could also use any type of squash, apart from, perhaps, spaghetti squash!

Put the stock in a suitable pot on the stove, next to where you will make the risotto, and keep it warm.

Heat half the butter in a large shallow pan, and fry the onion for about 10 minutes, until softened a little. Add the grated pumpkin and fry for 5 minutes. Add the rice and stir around to coat each grain with fat. Pour in the wine, and let this evaporate for a couple of minutes. Now start adding the hot stock in ladlefuls. Start to stir, and as soon as the first lot of liquid is absorbed, add some more, but not enough to drown it. Repeat for about 15–20 minutes – stirring and adding stock – which is when you should taste a grain of rice for your preferred *al dente* texture. Keep the rice moist but not too wet.

Add the rest of the butter, the nutmeg and cinnamon, and season to taste with salt and pepper. Add the Parmesan and parsley and stir in. Serve. Sprinkle with additional Parmesan if required.

SERVES 4

—1.5 litres (2¾ pints / 6 cups) vegetable stock
—80g (2¾oz) unsalted butter
—1 medium onion, peeled, finely sliced and chopped
—200g (7oz) pumpkin flesh, finely grated
—300g (10½oz / 1½ cups) risotto rice, such as *vialone nano* or *carnaroli*
—125ml (4fl oz / ½ cup) dry white wine
—½ teaspoon freshly grated nutmeg
—a pinch of ground cinnamon
—50g (1¾oz) Parmesan, freshly grated
—2 tablespoons finely chopped fresh flat-leaf parsley
—salt and freshly ground black pepper

# ZUCCA IN AGRODOLCE
*Sweet and Sour Pumpkin*

This is quite a rewarding pickle, which can be used to accompany cooked food, but can also be served by itself, as a little *antipasto*, or part of an *antipasto*. The natural sweetness of the pumpkin married with the slight sourness of the vinegar makes it very appetizing.

Peel the pumpkin and cut it first into 10cm (4 inch) sections, then into thin slices. Dust these with flour. Add enough olive oil to a medium frying pan so it is 1cm (¹/₂ inch) deep. Place over a medium heat. Fry the pumpkin slices until golden on both sides. Drain on absorbent kitchen paper.

In a ceramic container, make layers of the pumpkin slices, interspersed with the sage leaves and rosemary needles.

Put the vinegar into a small pan along with the garlic and some salt and pepper. Briefly bring to the boil.

Pour the hot vinegar over the layers of pumpkin in the container. Leave for a few hours for the flavours to combine before serving.

SERVES 4–6

—750g (1lb 10oz) yellow-orange
  pumpkin, with skin
—plain flour (all-purpose flour),
  for dusting
—olive oil, for shallow-frying
—6 large fresh sage leaves
—1 teaspoon rosemary needles
—50ml (2fl oz/¹/₄ cup) balsamic vinegar
—2 garlic cloves, peeled and finely
  chopped
—salt and freshly ground black pepper

# TORTELLI DI ZUCCA
## *Pumpkin Ravioli*

The most interesting peculiarity of this recipe comes from the use of the sweet amaretti biscuits and the pugency of the mostarda di Cremona, caramelized fruits in mustard syrup.

Preheat the oven to 200°C (400°F/gas 6).

Start the filling. Put the pumpkin flesh on a baking sheet, drizzle with a little olive oil, and bake in the preheated oven for about 50 minutes.

Meanwhile, make the pasta. Sift the flour on to a work surface and form into a mound with a well in the centre. Break the eggs into the well, and add the salt. Mix the eggs into the flour with your hands, until you have a coarse paste. Scrape up any sticky bits with a spatula, and add a little more flour if necessary. Clean the work surface before starting to knead. Knead the dough for 10–15 minutes – yes, sorry, it needs that time! – until the consistency is smooth and elastic. Wrap the dough in clingfilm(plastic wrap) and rest it in a cool place for 30 minutes.

The baked pumpkin should be soft and cooked, but not wet. If it still looks a little wet, wrap it in a clean cloth and squeeze to get as much liquid out as you can. Put the pumpkin flesh into a bowl and reduce it to a pulp with a fork. Add the chopped *mostarda*, the eggs, Parmesan, breadcrumbs, amaretti crumbs, and salt, pepper and nutmeg to taste. Stir to amalgamate everything – you should have a solid paste.

Unwrap the pasta dough and roll it out on a lightly floured surface to thin sheets, 5mm (¼ inch) thick (a machine will do this easily for you!). Cut these into bands 8cm (3¼ inches) wide. Place 1 teaspoon of the filling mixture every 6–7cm

—200g (7oz/1¼ cups) Italian '00' flour, sifted
—2 medium eggs
—a pinch of salt

### FILLING
—1.3kg (3lb) pumpkin flesh, after skinning and deseeding
—extra virgin olive oil
—1 tablespoon of mustard fruits (*mostarda di Cremona*), very finely chopped
—2–3 medium eggs, beaten
—100g (3½oz) Parmesan, freshly grated
—100g (3½oz/1 cup) dried white breadcrumbs
—4 amaretti biscuits, crumbled
—salt and freshly ground black pepper
—freshly grated nutmeg

### TO SERVE
—60g (2¼oz) unsalted butter
—4 tablespoons chopped fresh sage leaves
—60g (2¼oz) Parmesan, freshly grated

($2^{1}/_{2}$–$2^{3}/_{4}$ inches) along the middle of one of the pasta bands. Brush around each pile of mixture with some water. Place another pasta band over the top to cover, and press all around each pile of mixture to get the air out and to make the pasta sheets adhere to each other. Using a serrated pastry or *ravioli* wheel, cut out each *tortello* to about 7cm ($2^{3}/_{4}$ inch) square. Cover with a tea-towel and leave to rest for a while.

When ready to cook, boil the *tortelli* in salted water for 5–6 minutes. Scoop them out, using a slotted spoon, and place in a warmed dish.

Meanwhile, melt the butter in a small pan, add the sage and gently fry for a minute or two. Pour this over the *tortelli*, and serve on individual hot plates, sprinkled with the Parmesan.

SERVES 6–8

# ZUPPA ESTIVA DI CETRIOLO E POMODORO
*Summer Cucumber and Tomato Soup*

I owned and ran the Neal Street Restaurant for twenty-six years, and every summer I always featured a cold and refreshing soup such as this one. It is one of my classic recipes – so sorry, if you have seen it before!

Put the cucumber, dill and some salt and pepper into a liquidizer and whiz until liquid and smooth. Mix in the cream. Chill in the refrigerator.

Whiz the skinned tomatoes in the liquidizer with the basil, onion, olive oil, and some salt and pepper to obtain a smooth mixture. Chill in the refrigerator.

To serve, pour a little of the cucumber soup into a deep soup plate and carefully pour the tomato soup into the centre. Drizzle some extra virgin olive oil over the top, then decorate with a few basil leaves.

SERVES 4

—2 large cucumbers, peeled and cut into chunks
—2 tablespoons finely chopped fresh dill
—3 tablespoons double cream (heavy cream)
—2 large beef tomatoes, skinned and chopped
—10 fresh basil leaves, plus extra for garnish
—1 small white onion, peeled and roughly chopped
—2 tablespoons extra virgin olive oil
—salt and freshly ground black pepper

# FIORI DI ZUCCHINI RIPIENI
## *Stuffed Courgette Flowers*

You can also use *fiori di zucca* (pumpkin flowers) in Italy, or if you grow pumpkins yourself, but I generally prefer the female flower of the courgette (zucchini), which is the one with the little courgette attached. Naturally you can also use the male courgette flower, which grows at the end of a thin stem.

For the stuffing, mix the ricotta to a paste with the Parmesan, chives, egg yolks, nutmeg, and salt and pepper to taste.

Spoon the paste into a piping bag and divide it between your flowers, filling them well. Work gently, as the flowers are very fragile.

In a large deep frying pan, add enough olive oil and sunflower oil so that the pan is a third full. Place over a medium heat.

For the batter, simply mix the eggs and flour together.

To test whether the oil has reached the perfect frying temperature, drop a small piece of bread in. If it fries and goes golden, the oil is ready.

Dip the stuffed courgette flowers, one by one, into the batter, allow to drip, then immediately lower into the hot oil. Repeat with a couple more, but do not cook more than four at a time. Cook for 2–3 minutes, or until crisp and golden. Drain on absorbent kitchen paper, while you coat and cook the remaining flowers.

Eat while hot, either as a starter or as part of a *fritto misto di vegetali*.

SERVES 4–8

—8 female or 12 male courgette (zucchini) flowers, nicely open (and the interior checked for insects)
—a mixture of olive oil and sunflower oil, for shallow-frying

STUFFING
—400g (14oz/1¾ cups) fresh, soft, possibly sheep's milk, ricotta cheese
—20g (¾oz) Parmesan, freshly grated
—a little bunch of fresh chives, finely chopped
—2 medium egg yolks
—freshly grated nutmeg
—salt and freshly ground black pepper

BATTER
—3 medium eggs, beaten
—3 tablespoons plain flour (all-purpose flour)

# PARMIGIANA DI ZUCCHINI (O MELANZANE)
## *Baked Courgette (or Aubergine) with Cheese*

Contrary to common belief, the original parmigiana, an aubergine (eggplant) and cheese bake, comes from Sicily and not Emilia-Romagna, but all of Italy cooks the dish with gusto, and it is vegetarian. Using courgettes (zucchini) makes for a lighter dish, as they absorb less oil.

This is delicious for a light lunch on a sunny Sunday and, although there is a lot of work involved, it is so worthwhile if you are feeding a crowd.

Make the tomato sauce first, as described on page 181.

Now take the slices of the chosen vegetable. Dip them first into flour and then into the beaten egg. Heat a mixture of olive oil and sunflower oil in a frying pan, to a depth of about 2cm (³/₄ inch). Working in batches, fry the vegetable slices until golden on both sides, some 5–8 minutes, then set aside on absorbent kitchen paper. Repeat until all the slices have been fried.

Preheat the oven to 200°C (400°F/gas 6).

To assemble the *parmigiana*, take a baking tray or baking dish of about 20 x 30cm (8 x 12 inches) and about 8–10cm (3–4 inches) deep. Spread some of the sauce in the base, and start to build up layers of vegetables and sliced cheese. Sprinkle with Parmesan, then add another layer of tomato sauce. Continue until you have used up all the ingredients, finishing with Parmesan.

Bake in the preheated oven for 30–35 minutes. Let it rest and cool for a while before you serve.

SERVES 8

—1kg (2lb 4oz) courgettes (zucchini), trimmed and cut lengthways into 8mm (³/₈ inch) slices, or 1kg (2lb 4oz) aubergines (eggplants), trimmed and cut lengthways into thick 1cm (¹/₂ inch) slices
—plain flour (all-purpose flour), for dusting
—3 large eggs, beaten
—a mixture of olive oil and sunflower oil, for shallow-frying
—600g (1lb 5oz) Taleggio cheese, cut into small chunks
—100g (3¹/₂oz) Parmesan, freshly grated

TO SERVE
—1 recipe of tomato sauce (see page 181)

# ZUCCHINI RIPIENI
*Stuffed Courgettes*

The filling here is the same as for the stuffed onions on page 133. When Italians produce these kind of dishes, they like to add variety.

Cut the courgettes lengthways in half, and scoop out the soft white centre flesh, leaving a boat-shaped shell. Chop the white flesh finely and fry it in olive oil with the crumbled meat of the sausage for about 10 minutes, to cook the meat. Leave to cool down.

Preheat the oven to 180°C (350°F/gas 4).

Add the remaining ingredients to the meat mixture, and season with salt and pepper to taste. Mix well, then stuff each courgette half with the mixture.

Place on a baking tray and drizzle with a little olive oil. Bake in the preheated oven for 20 minutes, or until crisp on top. Eat hot or cold.

SERVES 4

—4 medium courgettes (zucchini), ends trimmed
—extra virgin olive oil

STUFFING
—the insides of the courgettes
—1 tablespoon extra virgin olive oil
—200g (7oz) *lucanica* sausage, meat removed from the skin
—1 tablespoon soft raisins
—1 tablespoon pine nuts
—freshly grated nutmeg
—a pinch of ground cinnamon
—3 tablespoons fresh breadcrumbs
—1 amaretti biscuit, crumbled
—1 tablespoon freshly grated Parmesan
—1 medium egg, beaten
—salt and freshly ground black pepper

*summer squashes*

# CAPONATA SICILIANA
## *Sicilian Vegetable Stew*

This is a recipe of which every Sicilian is proud. It actually has dual origin historically, coming from the French and Arab culinary traditions, when both occupied the island – at separate times – centuries ago. The French *ratatouille,* another aubergine (eggplant) stew, is very similar, and the capers and olives are the Arabic contribution. Whatever the origin, *caponata* is wonderful eaten hot or cold as an *antipasto* or side dish, or with bread as a snack.

Trim the aubergines, then cut into 2cm (³/₄ inch) square cubes. Blanch the celery, leaves and all, in boiling water for a minute or two, then drain and cut into small chunks of the same size. Chop the tomatoes into similar dice.

Heat the olive oil in a frying pan and fry the aubergine cubes until soft and brownish, about 15 minutes. Remove from the pan and set aside.

Put the celery, tomatoes, capers and olives into the pan and fry in any remaining oil to soften them, about 8–9 minutes. Add the aubergine, sugar and vinegar, with some salt and pepper to taste. Let the fumes of the vinegar evaporate while you stir for a few minutes, then the *caponata* is ready. Serve hot or cold.

SERVES 4–6

—4 large aubergines (eggplants)
—3 celery stalks
—4 ripe tomatoes
—6 tablespoons extra virgin olive oil
—2 tablespoons salted capers, desalted (see page 75)
—200g (7oz) pitted green olives
—1 tablespoon caster sugar (superfine sugar)
—2 tablespoons white wine vinegar
—salt and freshly ground black pepper

# MELANZANE SOTT'ACETO
## *Pickled Aubergine*

In the south of Italy, the cuisine is characterized by the wonderful vegetables that they can grow. They cook them there in an infinite number of ways, but I don't know of any Pugliese or Calabrian who wouldn't eat this as an *antipasto*. In season, they have so many aubergines (eggplants) that they have to find some way of using them up.

Not long ago I was in Australia, and one day a member of the public came up to me and presented me with a little jar. She said, 'My mother made this specially for you.' And it was this aubergine pickle…

You could add chilli to this if you like, which adds an interesting piquancy. Just make sure that it is cooked and preserved like the aubergine and garlic.

—2kg (4lb 8oz) aubergines (eggplants), trimmed and peeled
—1.5 litres (2¾ pints/6 cups) very good white wine vinegar
—4–6 large garlic cloves, peeled
—salt and freshly ground black pepper
—extra virgin olive oil, as required
—1 tablespoon dried oregano
—a few salted capers, desalted (see page 75) and finely chopped

Prepare the aubergines. Cut them into lengthways slices 3cm (1¼ inches) thick. Then cut each slice into 3cm (1¼ inch) thick strips.

Pour the vinegar and the same amount of water into a large saucepan, and add the aubergine, garlic and 10g (¼oz) of salt. Bring to the boil, then cook at a simmer for about 8 minutes. The aubergine strips should not be too soft. Drain and leave to cool. Discard the liquid, but keep the garlic.

Squeeze some of the excess liquid out of the aubergine strips, then put them into a bowl. Mix them with enough olive oil just to coat, along with the oregano and capers.

Put the aubergines and garlic into sterilized jars (see page 143 for how to sterilize). Cover everything with extra virgin olive oil. You can keep this for some time.

FILLS 4 X 400G (14OZ) JARS

# POLPETTE DI CARNE E MELANZANE
*Meat and Aubergine Rissoles*

*When my mother used to make polpette di carne e melanzane, plenty of hungry children were hanging around in the kitchen. These little rissoles are so simple, but so good!*

Cook the aubergines in slightly salted boiling water until not completely soft, about 10–15 minutes. Drain well and leave to cool. Squeeze to get rid of any water. Chop the aubergines finely.

Mix the chopped aubergines with the meat, Parmesan, eggs, garlic, breadcrumbs and parsley. Season with salt, pepper and nutmeg to taste.

Form the mixture into 24 small rounds, and slightly flatten them for the traditional rissole shape. Shallow-fry in batches in hot olive oil until brown on each side. Drain on absorbent kitchen paper, and keep warm in a low oven while you fry the rest.

Serve hot, either as a snack or a light lunch with a salad.

MAKES 24 RISSOLES

- 1kg (2lb 4oz) aubergines (eggplants), cut into quarters
- 500g (1lb 2oz) minced veal
- 40g (1½oz) Parmesan, freshly grated
- 2 large eggs, beaten
- 1 large garlic clove, peeled and very finely chopped
- 4 tablespoons fresh white breadcrumbs
- 2 tablespoons finely chopped fresh flat-leaf parsley
- freshly grated nutmeg
- olive oil, for shallow-frying
- salt and freshly ground black pepper

## AVOCADO PERA E GAMBERETTI
### *Avocado Stuffed with Prawns*

When I first came to London in 1975, the Italian food served was very surprising to me. There seemed to be various dishes that were completely unfamiliar: they did not exist in Italy, but had been adapted by and for the local population. Almost every restaurant offered *avocado e gamberetti,* and even today there are nostalgic people who would like to have it back on the menu… So here it is!

Peel and halve the avocados, and remove the stones. If not using straight away, brush the cut surfaces with a little lemon juice.

Mix the prawns with the mayonnaise and tomato purée, and season with salt and pepper to taste. Divide this between the cavities in the avocado halves.

Divide the lettuce between four serving plates, and place an avocado half on top of each. Serve with *grissini* (breadsticks).

SERVES 4

—2 large ripe avocados
—a little lemon juice
—1 head of little gem lettuce, cut into
  fine ribbons

FILLING
—120g (4¹/₄oz) peeled and cooked
  prawns (shrimp)
—6 tablespoons home-made
  mayonnaise (see page 000)
  or equivalent
—1 tablespoon tomato purée
—salt and freshly ground black pepper

# FRITTATA DI PEPERONI E MANDORLE
## *Pepper Omelette with Almonds*

A very simple dish like the *frittata* can be boring or excellent, depending on how you do it. This one has peppers as its base, cooked the Pugliese way, and it can be served as a side vegetable, a starter or indeed a main course with a good accompanying salad.

Cut the peppers in half, remove and discard the seeds, then cut the flesh into ribbons. Heat about half the olive oil in a high-sided 25cm (10 inch) frying pan, and fry these pepper ribbons until they are soft and starting to caramelize. Add the garlic halfway through the cooking and stir occasionally. Add the almonds, and salt and pepper to taste, as well as the sugar and vinegar. Stir together for a minute to let the fumes of the vinegar evaporate a little.

Beat the eggs in a large bowl, and stir in the Parmesan and a little salt.

Pour a little more olive oil into the pan, then add the egg mixture. Cook gently, to let it solidify and brown on one side, about 10 minutes. Every now and again use a spatula to gently loosen the bottom of the omelette from the sides, which allows some of the liquid mixture to hit the base of the pan and set. When there is no more liquid left, put a plate over the top of the pan and invert the omelette on to the plate, then slide it back into the pan, uncooked side down. Add the remaining oil, and brown the other side, about 5–6 minutes.

Cut into slices and serve, hot or cold.

SERVES 6, OR 4 IF GREEDY!

—3 large red or yellow peppers
—6 tablespoons extra virgin olive oil
—2 garlic cloves, peeled and sliced
—50g (1¾oz) flaked almonds (slivered almonds)
—1 tablespoon caster sugar (superfine sugar)
—2 tablespoons white wine vinegar
—10 medium eggs
—50g (1¾oz) Parmesan, freshly grated
—salt and freshly ground black pepper

*bush and tree fruit*

# PEPERONI AL FORNO CON BAGNA CAUDA
*Oven-baked Peppers with Anchovy Sauce*

Peppers and anchovies are a very important element of Piedmontese cooking. *Bagna cauda*, the famous Piedmontese 'hot dip', is usually served warm in the centre of the table – or in individual pots – for people to dip pieces of raw vegetable in. Here the dip is served in a slightly different way. I have made it slightly milder too, which suits the pepper perfectly, resulting in an excellent *antipasto*.

To make the original *bagna cauda* (which is much stronger), melt butter and oil and add the garlic and anchovies, to melt as well.

Preheat the oven to 200°C (400°F/gas 6).

Line a suitable baking tray with foil. Place the peppers on the foil, drizzle with a little olive oil, then roast in the preheated oven for 15–20 minutes.

Meanwhile, make the *bagna cauda*. Put the butter into a small pan with the garlic and milk and cook until the garlic dissolves or is very soft. Mash it to a paste, and stir to mix well. Add the anchovy fillets, and slowly let them dissolve. Mash these too a little if necessary. You should have a smoothish sauce/dip.

Place a tablespoonful of the sauce in each pepper half, and serve hot.

SERVES 4

—4 large red or yellow meaty peppers, quartered and deseeded
—extra virgin olive oil

BAGNA CAUDA
—50g (1¾oz) unsalted butter
—6 garlic cloves, peeled
—200ml (7fl oz/just over ¾ cup) milk
—10 anchovy fillets in oil, drained

# INSALATA DI PEPERONI ARROSTITI
*Salad of Grilled Peppers*

This recipe, common to the whole of the south of Italy, and now spreading worldwide, is one of my favourites. When I was a young man, still living at home, it was a great pleasure to come home late at night and find some leftover pepper salad to have as a delicious midnight feast.

Blacken the peppers, preferably over a charcoal grill, or in a very hot oven (220°C/425°F/gas 7). When the skin has blackened, remove the peppers from the grill or oven and leave to cool. When cool, remove the skin and seeds, retaining any juices, and slice the peppers into 2.5cm (1 inch) strips or thereabouts.

To the peppers and their juices, add the garlic (sliced coarsely it will be visible and you can avoid eating it!) or garlic oil, salt, parsley and olive oil and mix well. Leave for a few hours to allow the flavours to develop, and eat as part of an *antipasto*.

SERVES 4

—2 red peppers
—2 yellow peppers
—1 garlic clove, peeled and coarsely sliced, or 1 teaspoon garlic oil
—sea salt
—1 tablespoon coarsely chopped fresh flat-leaf parsley
—4 tablespoons extra virgin olive oil

## FRIARIELLI IN PADELLA
### *Fried Peppers*

There is a little confusion about *friarielli*. In Naples it is the tops of rape that go by this name, while in other parts of the south it is small green sweet peppers, which in Europe are known as Padrón peppers. These peppers, which came originally from the province of Padrón in Galicia, Spain, are mild and flavourful.

The little fried peppers are eaten either as a side dish or as a snack to accompany drinks.

Heat the oil in a frying pan, then add the peppers and fry on a moderate heat until they are brownish on each side. Add the sliced garlic and fry a little, then add the cherry tomato halves and the torn basil leaves.

Add the salt at the end and eat all of the peppers, seeds included, except for the stalks. Take care, though, that you use small sweet peppers, and not chillies!

SERVES 4

—425g (15oz) green Padrón peppers
—2 tablespoons extra virgin olive oil
—2 garlic cloves, peeled and sliced
—3 cherry tomatoes, halved
—a few fresh basil leaves, torn
—salt

# SPAGHETTI ARRABBIATA CON 'NDUJA
## *Spaghetti with Hot Chilli Pepper Paste*

*'Nduja* is a super-hot, spreadable salami, made from chilli and pork pieces and fat, to be either spread on *crostini* or used as spice in all sorts of dishes. This Calabrian speciality is delicious in a hot *arrabbiata* sauce, which I serve here with spaghetti.

Heat the olive oil in a large saucepan, then add the garlic and fry gently for about 5 minutes. Add the tomatoes and *'nduja*, and cook gently for another 20 minutes.

Meanwhile, cook the spaghetti in boiling salted water for 7 minutes or according to the packet instructions.

Drain the pasta and add to the sauce. Mix well, and add salt to taste. Divide between hot plates, and sprinkle with the cheese.

SERVES 4

—350g (12oz) spaghetti
—50g (1¾oz) Pecorino cheese, freshly grated
—salt and freshly ground black pepper

SAUCE
—6 tablespoons extra virgin olive oil
—1 garlic clove, peeled and finely chopped
—1 x 400g (14oz) tin of chopped tomatoes
—50g (1¾oz) *'nduja*

PEPERONI FARCITI
*Stuffed Peppers*
*Page 175*

# PEPERONI FARCITI
*Stuffed Peppers*

I always use red or yellow peppers because of their tenderness and flavour. Green peppers, when cooked, have a greasy taste, I feel, and I prefer to use them in other recipes. Piedmont is the region where the pepper is particularly celebrated: in Carmagnola they have a pepper festival every year. In 2010, they got into the *Guinness Book of Records* by making the largest *peperonata* ever…

Aubergines (eggplants) can be stuffed and cooked in the same way. Cut three medium aubergines in half, carve out some of the flesh in each half, and fry this in some olive oil until soft. Add to the stuffing below, mix, then stuff the aubergine halves, and bake as below.

Preheat the oven to 180°C (350°F/gas 4).

Cut the peppers in half from top to bottom and discard the seeds.

Soak the breadcrumbs in enough water to cover, then squeeze out the excess water. Mix the breadcrumbs with the capers, olives, tomatoes, garlic, parsley, anchovies and half the olive oil. Season with salt and pepper to taste. Mix well. Divide the stuffing between the pepper halves.

Place the peppers on a baking sheet and sprinkle with the remaining oil. Bake in the preheated oven for 30 minutes, until you see the edges of the peppers browning and a crisp crust building on top. They are excellent hot or cold.

SERVES 6

—3 large yellow or red peppers, or a mixture

STUFFING
—250g (9oz/5 cups) fresh white breadcrumbs
—1 tablespoon salted capers, desalted (see page 75)
—1 tablespoon finely chopped pitted black olives
—3 large tomatoes, skinned, deseeded and finely diced
—1 garlic clove, peeled and finely chopped
—2 tablespoons chopped fresh flat-leaf parsley
—4 anchovy fillets in oil, drained and finely chopped
—125ml (4fl oz/½ cup) extra virgin olive oil
—salt and freshly ground black pepper

*bush and tree fruit*

**175**

# SOFFRITTO DI MAIALE
## *Pork Offal Stew*

Winter, in our family, was never less exciting than the rest of the year as far as food was concerned. My mother always had something up her sleeve to make the family happy. Just before December the slaughter of the pigs was an annual happening at the local farm, and we were always given a tray of offal, which could be used immediately fresh, or turned into different specialities after freezing.

Clean and trim the offal. Cut the liver and kidneys into small pieces, the lung (or veal sweetbreads) into small chunks.

Heat the lard in a large saucepan and fry the onion, garlic and chillies for 5–10 minutes. Add all the pieces of offal, and let them brown on each side for about 5 minutes or so. (You may need to do this in batches.) Add the tomato purée, bay leaves and 400ml (14fl oz/1¾ cups) of water, then cover with the lid. Cook at a gentle simmer for 2 hours, adding some more water if necessary, and stirring every now and again.

When the mixture is tender, taste for seasoning. Either serve straight away – on toasted thick slices of country bread – or let it cool down and divide between small containers to freeze. When needed you can defrost only the amount required, put it into a pan with a little stock, and serve as above, on country bread.

SERVES 4

- 1kg (2lb 4oz) pork liver
- 3 pig's kidneys
- 400g (14oz) pork lung or, alternatively, veal sweetbreads
- 200g (7oz) lard, or 200ml (7fl oz/just over ¾ cup) olive oil
- 1 onion, peeled and finely chopped
- 2 garlic cloves, peeled and crushed
- 2 hot chillies, diced
- 1 x 300g (10½oz) jar of tomato purée
- 8 fresh bay leaves
- salt and freshly ground black pepper

*bush and tree fruit*

# OLIVE ALL'ASCOLANA
*Stuffed Olives from Ascoli*

The Marche, a region on the Adriatic coast between Emilia-Romagna and Abruzzi, is a well-known source of good chefs, good food and good wines. Various specialities appear regularly on the local menus, and one of them is the unique dish called olive all'Ascolana: these are giant olives, stoned and stuffed and fried, which are very welcome with an aperitif or offered at parties as finger food.

To start the stuffing, heat the butter in a large pan. Add the two minced meats and cook for a few minutes, then add the lemon zest and nutmeg. When the meat starts to brown, add the wine, tomato purée, and salt and pepper to taste, then cook gently for 30–40 minutes. Leave to cool.

When the mixture is cold, add the salami and mortadella, along with the truffle (if using), parsley, Parmesan and egg, and mix well. Blend the mixture in a blender to obtain a fairly soft paste that still has a little texture.

With a very sharp curved knife, cut out the stone from the olive by cutting the pulp in an ellipse to leave a spiral; it should open up like a continuous strip. Take a little of the filling and put it into the centre of the olive, which you then reshape into a large olive. Do this to all the olives, using up the stuffing.

Put the flour in one bowl, the beaten egg in another, and the breadcrumbs in a third. Dip the stuffed olives into the flour, then into the beaten egg, and finally into the crumbs.

Heat some olive oil in a small saucepan until hot enough to deep-fry, and deep-fry the olives in batches until golden brown. Drain and repeat until you have fried all the olives. Serve either hot – sprinkled with lemon juice – or cold.

FOR 30 OLIVES

- 30 very large green olives
- plain flour (all-purpose flour), for dusting
- 3 medium eggs, beaten
- fresh white breadcrumbs, for coating
- olive oil, for deep-frying
- lemon juice, for sprinkling

STUFFING
- 50g (1¾oz) unsalted butter
- 150g (5½oz) minced lean pork
- 150g (5½oz) minced beef
- finely grated zest of ½ a lemon
- freshly grated nutmeg
- 75ml (2½fl oz/⅜ cup) dry white wine
- 1 heaped teaspoon tomato purée
- 50g (1¾oz) salami, very finely chopped
- 30g (1oz) mortadella, very finely chopped
- 20g (¾oz) black truffle, cut into fine shavings (optional)
- 2 tablespoons chopped fresh flat-leaf parsley
- 30g (1oz) Parmesan, freshly grated
- 1 medium egg, beaten
- salt and freshly ground black pepper

## FRITTELLE DI POMODORI SECCHI
*Sun-dried or Oven-dried Tomato Fritters*

Sun-dried or otherwise-dried tomatoes have a much more intense taste than when raw. Dried tomatoes are usually found in *antipasti*, as pickles, as a snack or as a flavouring of soups and sauces. I fry them as fritters, and the result is magic, to be served with drinks.

For the batter, simply mix the eggs and flour together in a bowl.

Heat some olive oil in a pan. Dip the tomato halves into the batter and fry in the hot olive oil until they are golden on both sides, a couple of minutes. Drain on absorbent kitchen paper and serve immediately.

MAKES 24 FRITTERS

—olive oil, for shallow-frying
—24 sun-dried tomato halves, softened in water or kept in oil, or even some softer sun-blush tomatoes

BATTER
—3 medium eggs, beaten
—3 tablespoons plain flour (all-purpose flour)

# SALSA BASE DI POMODORO
*Basic Tomato Sauce*

In Italian markets, in season, you will find ripe tomatoes on sale specifically for sauce. They are locally grown and newly picked, and are called *pomodori da sugo*. They are full of natural elements such as vitamins and, because they are ripe and not acid, they are ideal for sauce. This basic tomato sauce is used for a variety of purposes: for a *ragù*, for pasta, for soups and potatoes, etc. Personally I like it very simply served, with lovely *spaghettini* and a scattering of basil leaves.

Put the olive oil into a large saucepan with the garlic or onion, and fry gently for 8–10 minutes to soften. Add the tomatoes and basil, with salt and pepper to taste. Let the sauce gently cook for 20 minutes, or longer if you want a more concentrated taste.

Use as required.

**MAKES ABOUT 700G (1LB 9OZ)**

## MARMELATA DI POMODORI VERDI
### *Green Tomato Jam*

This concoction came about after a friend told me his garden, towards the end of the season, was full of green tomatoes that he could not use. He gave them to me, and I decided not to make pickle or fritters, as many people do, but a sweet marmalade or jam. It is delicious!

You will need to 'test for a set'. Put three saucers into the freezer before you start, and when you reach the point of testing, take the pan off the heat, and put a spoonful of the jam on to one of the cold saucers. If it wrinkles, after a minute, when you push it with a finger, it is ready. If it is still runny, bring the jam back to the simmer, and test again a few minutes later.

Cut the tomatoes into little chunks and put them into a large preserving pan with 2–3 tablespoons of water. Bring slowly to the boil, and continue simmering over a very low heat for 20–30 minutes.

Meanwhile, finely grate the rind from the lemons. Squeeze the juice, and save the pips, tying them up in a little muslin bag.

Add the lemon rind, juice and muslin bag to the tomatoes, along with the spices, salt and about the same amount of water as above. Stir until amalgamated, then pour in the sugar and let it dissolve over a low heat. Stirring occasionally to prevent sticking, carry on cooking gently until the mixture has reduced in volume by one-third.

Test for a set (see above), put into sterilized jars (see page 143), then seal and store in a cool dry place.

**MAKES 2KG (4LB 8 OZ)**

—2kg (4lb 8oz) green tomatoes
—3 lemons
—1 teaspoon ground cinnamon
—½ teaspoon freshly grated nutmeg
—½ teaspoon ground cloves
—a pinch of salt
—2kg (4lb 8oz) preserving sugar

# GRANDE PASTICCIO
*The Great Lamb Pie*

This is the Italian version of moussaka. A simpler dish is made in the south of Italy in the region of Puglia, where part of the population speaks Greek, and still has some culinary culture reminding them of the old country. This is the predecessor of the *parmigiana di melanzane* from Sicily.

Heat some olive oil in a deep-frying pan or deep-fryer. Deep-fry the large slices of potato, aubergine and courgette in batches until nearly cooked, then set aside on absorbent kitchen paper.

Make the *ragù* filling next. Heat 6 tablespoons of olive oil in a large pan, and fry the garlic for a minute or two. Add the mince and stir well, letting it brown. When it is uniformly brown, add the tomatoes, bay leaves and cinnamon and stir-fry for a few minutes. Season with salt and pepper, then put a lid on and leave to braise for 30 minutes.

Preheat the oven to 200°C (400°F/gas 6).

Meanwhile, make the béchamel sauce. Melt the butter in a medium pan, then stir in the flour until smooth. Pour in a little milk at a time, stirring constantly, until all the milk has been added, and the sauce is smooth. Season with salt and pepper to taste, and leave it to cool.

Now assemble the pie. Use a large pie dish of at least 7.5cm (2½ inches) in depth. Grease it with a little olive oil, then put in a layer of fried potato topped with some of the *ragù*. Top this with the fried aubergine, then some more *ragù*. Finally, put the fried courgette on top with a layer of the remaining *ragù*. Top the lot with the béchamel sauce, smoothing it gently over everything. Sprinkle with the grated cheese.

Bake in the preheated oven for 30 minutes. Let it rest briefly before serving, perhaps with a green salad.

SERVES 8 OR MORE

—olive oil, for deep-frying
—2 large potatoes, about 600g (1lb 5oz), peeled and thickly sliced
—2 large aubergines (eggplants), about 485g (1lb 1oz), trimmed and thickly sliced
—2 large courgettes (zucchini), about 400g (14oz), trimmed and thickly sliced
—200g (7oz) Gruyère cheese, grated

FILLING
—extra virgin olive oil
—4–5 garlic cloves, peeled and chopped
—2kg (4lb 8oz) lean minced lamb (ground lamb)
—600g (1lb 5oz) tomatoes, coarsely chopped to a pulp, or the equivalent of tinned chopped tomatoes
—2 bay leaves
—1 cinnamon stick
—salt and plenty of freshly ground black pepper

BÉCHAMEL SAUCE
—200g (7oz) unsalted butter
—150g (5½oz/1 cup) plain flour (all-purpose flour)
—2 litres (3½ pints/8 cups) milk

*bush and tree fruit*

# POMODORI FARCITI
## *Stuffed Tomatoes*

Tomatoes, together with other stuffed vegetable recipes (see pages 133, 159 and 177), are very much a must in the summer. Sometimes they are stuffed with rice and mint, but I like them with breadcrumbs.

Preheat the oven to 200°C (400°F/gas 6).

Cut the top off each tomato and set aside. Spoon the seeds and pulp into a bowl. Mix with the breadcrumbs, mint, garlic, capers and 3 tablespoons of olive oil. Add salt and pepper to taste.

Stuff the tomatoes with this mixture, and place them on a baking tray. Top with their cut-off 'hats'.

Sprinkle with a little olive oil and bake in the preheated oven for 25–30 minutes. These are good hot or cold.

SERVES 4

—4 very large, ripe tomatoes

STUFFING
—pulp and seeds from the tomatoes
—100g (3½oz/2 cups) fresh white breadcrumbs
—2 tablespoons chopped fresh mint
—2 garlic cloves, peeled and very finely chopped
—1 tablespoon salted capers, desalted (see page 75)
—extra virgin olive oil
—salt and freshly ground black pepper

# PANZANELLA
## *Bread and Tomato Salad*

It is summer, you have some stale bread and a few fresh ingredients. That is all you need for *panzanella,* which is quick, refreshing and wholesome as a starter or snack celebrating the tomato.

Put the dried bread into a bowl, and pour over just enough water to soften it, for a few minutes only. Reduce the pieces of bread to large chunks, and get rid of any surplus water in the bowl.

Add the tomatoes and their juices, the celery, onion, green pepper, olives and chopped basil. Mix well and then add the olive oil, vinegar and garlic, with some salt and pepper to taste. Mix again until a juicy mixture results, and divide between serving plates. Serve garnished with a sprig of basil.

SERVES 4 OR MORE

—500g (1lb 2oz) stale white or brown bread, dried in the oven until golden
—600g (1lb 5oz) ripe tomatoes, cut into small chunks (save all the juices)
—50g (1¾oz) celery stalks, trimmed and finely chopped
—1 small onion, peeled and finely sliced
—1 green pepper, deseeded and finely sliced
—a few pitted black olives
—2 tablespoons chopped fresh basil, plus a few sprigs to garnish
—6 tablespoons extra virgin olive oil
—1 tablespoon white wine vinegar
—1 large garlic clove, peeled and crushed
—salt and freshly ground black pepper

PULSES
AND GRAINS

We have already talked about pods and seeds, and in this section we are going to be talking about seeds again, but on the whole those that are used dried rather than fresh. Both pulses and grains produce seeds that are food for human or animal consumption. In fact, many experts call both of these seed-producing plants 'grain crops', and they are classified into several types: the cereal grains such as wheat and rye (which are members of the grass family); the pseudo-cereal grains such as buckwheat (no true relation to wheat or other cereal grains); the legume or pulse grains such as beans and peas; and the oilseeds, grains which are grown mostly for their oil, such as rapeseed.

Pulses and grains are among the most ancient of foods. The first crops were thought to have been domesticated around 9,000 BC in the 'Fertile Crescent' of the Middle East, between the Euphrates and Tigris rivers, evidenced by cave and other drawings, archaeological discoveries and grave goods. Because grain needed to be grown, cared for and harvested on a seasonal basis, grain agriculture could probably have led to the first settlements, to the transition from a hunter-gatherer society to a settled agricultural society – in other words, the beginnings of civilization. When the fresh grains or pulses were dried, they were able to be stored through the winter, providing nourishment when fresh foods were scarce or non-existent, and they could easily be transported, so they were probably the most valuable of foods.

Also contributing to their value is the fact that both types of crop are very rich in nutrition. Grains, pulses and seeds are packed with all the energy and nutrients needed for the next generation of plants, and so can form the chief source of energy (carbohydrate) for the majority of the world's population. Although pulses are also rich in protein (thus can take the place of meat for vegetarians), this protein is incomplete, but eating pulses in tandem with grains creates a good nutritional balance.

I would love to do proper research regarding all these foods, but it would take years and years, and for that I would have to live for ever…

# PULSES

Legumes or leguminous plants are a group of vegetable plants that produce pods containing seeds. Some of these seeds are edible fresh, pod and all, before the seed is ripe (runner beans, mangetout or snowpeas); some have seeds that are eaten when podded or shelled (broad beans or fava beans); and some of these seeds are left to mature in the pod and then dried. These latter are what we call pulses, and include dried beans of all types, peas, lentils and chickpeas. Before we start describing them, please remember when cooking any pulse, you should not add salt, as this will toughen their skins. Season to taste only when the pulses are fully cooked.

A poetic naturalist said to me one day that when a small child passes wind, the soul of a bean goes to heaven! Having lived in Germany for many years, I also remember the phrase – which is obviously intended for children – that '*Jedes Böhnchen gibt ein Tönchen*' (every little bean makes its own sound), referring to the flatulence that many beans cause. **Dried beans** (*fagioli*) may be the noisiest of vegetables, but they are also an important part of the Italian diet, because of their high protein, vitamin and mineral content, and their fibre. Every region in Italy has a different dish, made from a different type of bean, whether *cannellini*, *borlotti*, *fava* or broad.

As mentioned in the pods and seeds section, the **broad bean** (*fava*) was the original European bean, and it is eaten both fresh and dried. The dried beans, if you can find them without skins (which are tough), are made in Sicily into a purée, *maccu*; a similar purée in Puglia is delicious with braised wild chicory (see my version on page 207).

Kidney and other beans were introduced to Italy and the rest of Europe after the discovery of the New World. The family of kidney beans include two that are very popular in Italy, *cannellini* and *borlotti*. Both can be found fresh, but are used mostly dried, the latter more popular in the north, the former in the south. ***Borlotti* beans** are cooked with brassica veg such as cabbage in filling winter soups, and in the famous *pasta e fagioli*, which is popular all over Italy. (*Borlotti* are also known as Saluggia beans, named after a town in Piedmont where they are prolifically grown.) ***Cannellini* beans** are also canned and bottled, and are used in a variety of soups, including *minestrone*, and salads. The Tuscans – known as 'bean-eaters' for fairly obvious reasons – cook them in a glass flask, *fagioli al fiasco*, and in Campania they are used in *pasta e fasuli* (the Neapolitan word for *fagioli*), which is celebrated in the song 'That's Amore'.

Other kidney beans include the French *flageolet*, red kidney bean (used in the Texan *chili con carne*), and butter or lima beans. Most of these dried beans need to be soaked overnight, or for at least 12 hours, before cooking. After draining and rinsing, most

of them need to be cooked at a good boil for 10 minutes, then simmered for about an hour until cooked and tender. All kidney beans are good cold in salads (see page 197).

**Soya beans** (*fagioli di soia*) have found their way to the Western dining table relatively late, only in the twentieth century. They are originally from China, where they were grown and eaten as long ago as 1,000 years BC. Soya beans are as near to a complete protein as a vegetable food can be, containing almost as many amino acids as red meat. Available fresh (known as *edamame*), dried, canned or frozen, soya beans are now one of the world's largest crops. The dried beans should be soaked overnight, cooked at a good boil for half an hour or so, then simmered for at least a couple of hours until tender. Commercially, soya is used to make many familiar products, such as flour, oil, *tofu*, TVP (textured vegetable protein) or *quorn*, and fermented for soy and tamari sauces and the *miso* paste so popular in Japanese cooking. Italy has become a major producer of soya beans because of its favourable climatic conditions.

**Peas** (*piselli*) have been a basic of the human diet since at least the Stone Age, but it was the dried pea that ruled. It was not until the Italians cultivated more tender varieties of pea in the sixteenth century that we grew to appreciate them fresh. We still eat them dried in Italy, though, as they are wonderful in soup, with some prosciutto (not too dissimilar to the English pea and ham soup), with potatoes or spare ribs. Cooked and puréed, they are a wonderful accompaniment to pork and other meat dishes: in Britain a dried pea purée, 'mushy peas', accompanies the traditional fish and chips. Dried peas need to be soaked before cooking.

The **chickpea** (*cece*) is a pulse native to India, south-west Asia and the Middle East. Also known as Bengal gram, the chickpea is as important in those areas as it is in Italy and Spain. It is almost never seen fresh, but comes from small fat pods containing two to three large seeds, which are dried. After soaking (for 8–24 hours, depending on age), the peas can be braised (for at least 3 hours), then used in a variety of ways. *Pasta e ceci* is a dish of chickpeas and pasta popular in the north of Italy. In Sardinia, Piedmont and Liguria, chickpeas are ground into flour which is made into a pancake-like flat bread, called *farinata* or *faina* (much the same as the *socca* of Nice). In Sicily you find *panelle*, which look like fried slices of polenta, but are fritters made with that same chickpea flour. I've also used chickpea flour to make *gnocchi*, which worked well. In the Middle East chickpeas are mashed to a purée, mixed with *tahini* (sesame seed paste), and made into the popular dip, *hummus. Cicerchie*, an old-fashioned pulse similar to chickpeas, is known as 'grass pea' in English. It is used in parts of Italy in the same way as chickpeas, and is popular in Spain as well. It contains toxins, though, so must be used with care.

The **lentil** (*lenticchia*) comes from South Asia, but has been cultivated in the Mediterranean area for at least 10,000 years. Like many other of the pulses, lentils are a winter staple, and a traditional accompaniment to the meats that were preserved for winter, such as bacon and ham, or indeed sausages. Lentils and sausages are popular throughout the north of the country, and in Emilia–Romagna, lentils are classically served with stuffed pigs' trotters or *zampone*.

There are various types of lentil: the Puy from France, the Castelluccio from Umbria in Italy, the red (usually split) and others from India and elsewhere in Asia (generically known as *dhal*). Castelluccio lentils are organically grown, and are very highly valued and priced; they are delicious braised and eaten hot, or cold in salads. Another delicious Italian lentil is the *lenticchia de Altamura*, from Puglia. Lentils do not need soaking like other pulses, but they do need a thorough wash, as they can be very dusty, and can contain tiny stones.

## GRAINS

The word 'cereal' comes from Ceres, the Roman goddess of corn. The term 'cereal grain' is used to describe any grain – or seed – from a domesticated grass, and includes the Old World cereal grains such as wheat, barley, millet, oats, rye and rice (and buckwheat, although this is *not* from a grass), and the New World maize and quinoa.

Grains, with **wheat** (*frumento* or *grano duro*) in pole position, are the most important basic foods, and they help to sustain the majority of the world's population. At one time soldiers were paid in salt and grain, with which they could barter for other goods, or produce bread. And for Italians even today, wheat means bread and, above all, pasta. To produce good pasta, the first necessity is a particular type of wheat, one that grows successfully in Italy (but is now supplied from elsewhere, as Italy cannot supply her own needs): this is commonly known as hard wheat, semolina or durum wheat (*Triticum durum*, or *grano duro*). Good pasta needs a hard 'durum' flour, because of its gluten content, which prevents the pasta stretching and breaking while it is drying, and also helps the pasta retain texture and flavour during its cooking. For, as you all know, pasta must remain '*al dente*', with a little resistance to the bite.

Durum wheat was developed from an ancient type of wheat called emmer (*T. dicoccum*). This is known in Italy as *farro*, and its popularity has led to the development of another wheat type, known as spelt (*T. spelta*). Einkorn (*T. monococcum*) is yet another ancient wheat, known as *farro piccolo* (little farro) in Italy. Spelt, emmer, einkorn and durum wheat flours are available from good delicatessens, as is soft wheat flour (*frumento*), made from *T. aestivum*, which is used for breads and cakes in Italy.

Semolina – ground durum wheat – is also used to make couscous (*cuscus*), soups and *gnocchi* (in particular the famous baked *gnocchi alla romana*). Couscous is not a grain in its own right, but is made from little pellets of semolina. In Morocco, it is steamed to accompany a spicy stew of meat or vegetables; flavoured and coloured with saffron, it is served in Sicily with a fish stew. *Fregola*, the Sardinian version of couscous, is toasted and served in soups or with fish or meat stews. *Bulgur* or *bulghar*, cracked wheat, is not used much in Italy, but it is the centrepiece of the popular Middle Eastern herb and cracked wheat salad, *tabbouleh*. And yet another wheat product, from the Middle East and North Africa, is *freekeh*, green wheat grains/seeds which have been roasted: these have a unique smoky flavour.

A special wheat dish made in Campania, especially for Easter, is '*pastiera di grano*'. The whole-wheat grain or berry is cooked in milk until soft and then combined with ricotta, cooked fruit and cinnamon, and baked in a shortcrust pastry shell (see page 223). At this time, housewives prepare many *pastieri* to give to friends and relatives for good luck. Wheat berries and flakes are also used for breakfast cereals, which have now been introduced to the Italian diet, as have cereals made from the other familiar grains, **rye** (*segale*), **barley** (*orzo*), **millet** (*miglio*) and **oats** (*avena*). None are used much nowadays in Italian cooking, as wheat, maize and rice seem to have taken over.

Being the staple food of most of Asia, **rice** (*riso*) is second only to wheat in importance so far as world nutrition is concerned. In Asia, there are various types such as basmati, sticky, glutinous, etc., and in America, Carolina used to produce long-grain rice, as do, to this day, Cajun farmers around New Orleans (also farming crayfish for the local *gumbo* in the flooded rice paddies). Wild rice, with its nutty black strands, comes from North America as well, a water grass distantly related to Asian rice.

Originally from China, rice has been cultivated mainly in the valley of the River Po in the north of Italy, because there it can enjoy the abundance of water coming from the Alps, which is channelled to the fields on either side of the river right through to the Veneto. The most famous type of rice grown and used in Italy is risotto rice: the best varieties include *carnaroli*, *arborio*, *roma* and *vialone nano*. These risotto rices have been developed to give the requisite and infinitely desirable creaminess to a finished risotto. (Lesser rice qualities are used for rice pudding, soups and other dishes.)

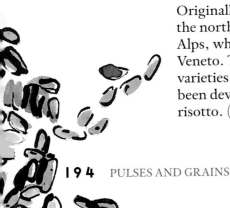

One rice that I particularly love is a very special one, grown in the province of Vercelli in the Po Valley. *Acquarello carnaroli* rice is grown exclusively by the Rondolino family, rice growers for many generations. It is a rice that is aged for up to nine years, and it is healthier than other rices as it retains its germ after husking. The family had a wonderful party once: they invited the great chefs of the world – belonging to an exclusive club called 'chefs of chefs of chefs' – as well as the great and the good from all over the world, and we were all together, Obama, the Queen, eating risotto in the Po Valley…

**Buckwheat** (*grano saraceno*) is not actually a grass like the other cereals, but because it is cultivated for its seeds, it is referred to as a 'pseudo-cereal'. It comes from Mongolia and has been cultivated for thousands of years; it was brought to Europe by the Moors, which explains its Italian name. A century ago, Russia was the world's greatest producer of buckwheat, thus the use of buckwheat flour in the famous *blinis*; the flour is also used in the *crêpes* of northern France. In Italy, buckwheat flour is used in the making of a special pasta and a coarse polenta. The pasta is called *pizzoccheri* (see page 212). Buckwheat is grown in only two areas of Italy, in the Valtellina in Lombardy, and in the Veneto.

**Maize** (*mais* or *granoturco*) came to Europe after the discovery of the Americas. It is a quick-growing grass native to South America, and was a staple food in ancient times. It is still the most widely grown cereal in the Americas today. There are two types of maize (or corn): sweetcorn – corn on the cob, popcorn, baby corn, etc. – and field corn, which is tougher and starchier, used for cornflour, corn oil and animal feed. In Europe we eat it straight from the cob, or as (tinned) sweetcorn kernels; in Italy, we make polenta from corn. Once chestnut flour was made into a sustaining porridge for the poor in the north of Italy; when maize arrived, it replaced the chestnut. Today polenta made from corn is having a revival in good restaurants, where it is served with juicy meat dishes. It can be flavoured with cheese, allowed to set, then sliced and fried as a savoury accompaniment. Maize flour can also be used in cakes and biscuits.

# INSALATA DI TUTTI FAGIOLI
*Multi-bean Salad*

Worldwide there is an infinite variety of pulses, and this salad is one exciting way of celebrating them. I leave the combination up to your culinary fantasy, mixing fresh with tinned or even frozen. To feed four to six people you will need about 350g (12oz) of dried beans, but as a rough guide, perhaps cook 50g (about 1¾oz) of each of seven different ones…

If you use dried pulses, soak them in cold water to cover overnight. Discard the soaking water and cook them in fresh water until tender for 1–2 hours, boiling for 10 minutes at the beginning of the cooking time. Season with salt only when cooked. If you use frozen items, just cook them in slightly salted water and drain. If you use tins or jars (that is the easiest), just drain them and use. The important thing is to have all the beans cooked and soft.

Preheat the oven to 180°C (350°F/gas 4). Put the garlic heads, still in the skin, on a piece of foil on a baking sheet, and drizzle with a little of the olive oil. Wrap in the foil and place in the preheated oven. Roast for 25 minutes.

When cool, squeeze the creamy, cooked garlic from the cloves into a large serving bowl. Add the remaining oil, the herbs, vinegar or lemon juice, salt and pepper, and the beans. Mix well. Serve hot or cold, with an extra sprinkle of chives.

SERVES 4–6

—350g (12oz) mixed dried beans (edamame or soya, red kidney, broad/fava, *cannellini*, *borlotti*, *flageolet*, black-eye, butter/lima, chickpeas)
—3 large garlic heads, kept in the skin
—6 tablespoons best extra virgin olive oil
—1 tablespoon each of chopped fresh basil, flat-leaf parsley, mint, sage and chives
—2 tablespoons white wine vinegar or lemon juice
—salt and freshly ground black pepper

*pulses*

# FAGIOLI GRASSI
*Stewed Fat Beans*

This is a filling winter dish which is served as a carnival food in Ivrea, a town in Piedmont, near to where I was brought up. The carnival takes place around the middle of February, before Lent, the lean Christian month that lasts until Easter. Historically, the rich used to give beans and grains to the poor people at this time, and allow them the use of ovens. They are called 'fat beans' because of the ingredients with which they are cooked (all that pork skin). The beans are very tasty and extremely nutritious, but perhaps not for the faint-hearted!

—2 tablespoons extra virgin olive oil
—2 large onions, peeled and coarsely chopped
—300g (10½oz) dried *borlotti* beans, soaked in cold water for 24 hours
—4–6 pieces of pork belly skin, each about 12–16cm (4½–6 inches), fat removed
—3 sprigs of fresh rosemary
—freshly grated nutmeg
—1 small bunch of fresh flat-leaf parsley, chopped
—6 pork cooking sausages
—2 tablespoons tomato purée
—salt and freshly ground black pepper

In a large saucepan, heat the olive oil to medium, and fry the onions until softened, about 10 minutes. Drain the beans and add them to the onions with 2 litres (3½ pints/8 cups) of fresh cold water. Bring to the boil and boil for about 10 minutes.

Lay the pieces of pork belly skin on a clean work surface, and sprinkle each with the needles from 2 of the rosemary sprigs, the black pepper, nutmeg and parsley. Roll up like a sausage, away from you, and secure three or four times with pieces of butcher's string. Add these little rolls to the beans, and cook at a simmer for 2 hours.

Now add the sausages, tomato purée and the final sprig of rosemary, and cook for another hour. Test to see if the pork skin and beans are soft; if not, cook for a little longer.

Add a little water if too dry, and some salt and pepper if required. Cut the pork belly skin rolls into slices, the sausages too if you like, and eat everything warm.

SERVES 4–6

# CANNELLINI, COZZE E VONGOLE
## *Cannellini Beans with Mussels and Clams*

Usually beans are eaten by themselves (often with rosemary and extra virgin olive oil), or with pork and vegetables. This is a rare combination with seafood, and it provides a particularly delicate taste. The recipe is cooked in two parts.

To start the beans, heat the olive oil in a medium pan and fry the garlic for a few minutes without letting it brown. Add the tomato, rosemary and drained beans and cook for about 5 minutes, just to warm the beans through.

To start the seafood, wash the shells well, discarding any that gape open.

Heat the olive oil in a large pan and fry the garlic and chilli for a few minutes, then add the mussels, clams and wine. Put a lid on and cook, shaking the pan from time to time until all the shells open, revealing the meat inside. Discard any shells that have not opened. Leave to cool, then discard most of the shells after having taken the meat, leaving some still with their shells for decoration.

Now mix the mussels, clams and parsley with the beans, and warm up slightly. Season with black pepper to taste. Serve on a plate with the sauce and eat with bread.

SERVES 4

### BEANS
—1 tablespoon extra virgin olive oil
—1 garlic clove, peeled and sliced
—1 ripe large tomato, deseeded and finely chopped
—1 sprig of fresh rosemary
—600g (1lb 5oz) tinned *cannellini* beans, drained (cooking dried beans takes longer)

### SEAFOOD
—1kg (2lb 4oz) mussels in the shell
—1kg (2lb 4oz) small clams in the shell
—1 tablespoon extra virgin olive oil
—1 garlic clove, peeled and sliced
—a pinch of dried chilli
—125ml (4fl oz/½ cup) white wine
—2 tablespoons chopped fresh flat-leaf parsley
—freshly ground black pepper

# PANELLE ALLA ROMANA
*Chickpea Gnocchi*

The inspiration for this dish was the Roman *gnocchi alla romana*, made with polenta or semolina. Here, though, instead of using semolina, I use chickpea flour. In Sicily, *panelle* are fritters made of chickpea flour, and these are sold between slices of bread or in a roll as a popular street food.

Chickpea flour can be found in many supermarkets, and in Indian grocers, as 'gram' or 'gram flour'. It is gluten-free, so is ideal for those who are wheat intolerant.

—6 tablespoons extra virgin olive oil
—400g (14oz/2½ cups) chickpea flour
—2 medium eggs, beaten
—freshly grated nutmeg
—60g (2¼oz) unsalted butter
—30g (1oz) Parmesan, freshly grated
—salt and freshly ground black pepper

Put 1.2 litres (2 pints/5 cups) of water into a large saucepan, add the olive oil and some salt, and bring to the boil. Pour the flour into the boiling water, using a large whisk to prevent lumps forming. Cook for 10 minutes, until the mixture is smooth, then let it cool down a little before adding the beaten eggs and a couple of grates of nutmeg. Stir well.

Pour on to a marble surface or other cold work surface and, using a spatula, spread the mixture out until it is evenly about 2cm (¾ inch) thick. (A tip: oil the spatula before you flatten the mixture, which will stop it sticking.) Leave to cool further.

Preheat the oven to 200°C (400°F/gas 6).

Now cut the cooled mixture into teardrops with a medium biscuit cutter. Butter a baking tray and lay the chickpea discs on it, slightly overlapping, like the tiles on a roof. Sprinkle with flakes of butter and the grated Parmesan.

Bake in the preheated oven for 15–20 minutes, until a golden crust forms on top. Serve as a starter, with some tomato sauce if you like.

SERVES 4

# FARINATA
*Chickpea Flatbread*

You will find this popular dish in the morning as a breakfast, anywhere in Liguria, Tuscany or even Sicily. The use of the chickpea flour is pretty obviously an ancient one, and the combination with the olive oil and the herb makes it a welcome snack at any time of day. Serve the bread with a stew of vegetables, or with a simple tomato sauce.

—400g (14oz/2¹/₂ cups) chickpea flour
—100ml (3¹/₂fl oz/just under ¹/₂ cup) extra virgin olive oil
—salt and freshly ground black pepper
—2 sprigs of fresh rosemary

In a large pan, mix 1.2 litres (2 pints/5 cups) of water and the flour together until smooth. Let it rest overnight at room temperature (but not perhaps if it is midsummer!).

Preheat the oven to 200°C (425°F/gas 7).

Before cooking, scoop away the foam that will have formed on top. Mix the liquid, then stir in the olive oil and some salt. Take a large baking tray about 4cm (1¹/₂ inches) deep, and cover the bottom by about 2.5cm (1 inch) with the liquid. Add the rosemary leaves, and lots of freshly ground black pepper.

Bake in the preheated oven for 15–20 minutes, until the flatbread has set and coloured a little. Remove the tray from the oven and cut the bread into squares or lozenges. Serve warm.

MAKES ENOUGH FOR QUITE A CROWD

## PASTA E CECI (LAGANE E TRIA)
### *Noodles and Chickpeas*

The first-century BC Roman poet Cato wrote in his *Sermones* that he was going home to have a meal of leeks and chickpeas mixed with what he called *laganum*. This was a basic pasta, probably cut into long lengths. To this day, in Puglia and elsewhere in the south, *ciceri* or *lagane e tria*, a soup of chickpeas, pasta (usually *tagliatelle*) and other vegetables (including potato!), is a popular speciality.

By using ready-cooked chickpeas from a tin, you avoid the lengthy business of soaking the chickpeas overnight and then boiling for hours. I tried it both ways, and there wasn't much difference. But if you want to do it properly, soak the dried chickpeas overnight in plenty of water, with some bicarbonate of soda, which helps soften the skins. Drain and cook in fresh water, on a medium heat, for 3 hours. Drain well.

Heat the olive oil in a large saucepan, add the onion, garlic and *prosciutto* and fry briefly. Add the potatoes and celery and about 2 litres (3½ pints/8 cups) of water. Bring to the boil and cook until the potato cubes are soft.

Add the pasta, salt to taste and the peppercorns, and cook until the pasta is to your taste (*al dente*, but not too much). Serve hot.

SERVES 4–6

— 200g (7oz) dried chickpeas, or 2 x 400g (14oz) tins of cooked chickpeas (garbanzo beans)
— 4 tablespoons extra virgin olive oil
— 1 small onion, peeled and finely chopped
— 2 garlic cloves, peeled and finely chopped
— 150g fatty *prosciutto*, chopped into chunks
— 2 medium potatoes, peeled and cut into small cubes
— 2 celery stalks, trimmed and cut into small pieces
— 300g (10½oz) very large *pappardelle* (3cm/1¼ inches wide, possibly home-made)
— salt
— 1 tablespoon black peppercorns

*pulses*

# MACCU CON CICORIA
*Broad Bean Purée with Chicory*

This is a Pugliese speciality of peasant origin, made with local ingredients. The highlight is the nutty sweetness of the purée, and the slight bitterness of the wild chicory that can be found in springtime in the fields. Instead of wild chicory I am using *catalogna* chicory, which belongs to the same chicory family, and has a pleasant bitterness. You could also use frisée or *radicchio*, if you like.

Soak the beans in cold water for 24 hours.

Discard the soaking water and, in a large saucepan, cover the beans with fresh water. Add the unpeeled garlic cloves and bring to the boil. Reduce the heat and simmer for 2 hours, until the beans break down into a purée. Stir from time to time to avoid sticking. Discard the garlic, and add a little olive oil. Season with salt and pepper to taste and keep warm.

Meanwhile, cook the chicory. For the *catalogna*, keep everything and use as it is. (If using radicchio, cut into large strips.) Heat 3 tablespoons of olive oil in another saucepan, and add the sliced garlic cloves and the chilli flakes. Gently fry for a few minutes. Add the *catalogna* or *radicchio*, with about 150ml (5fl oz/²/₃ cup) of water, and cook, lid on, until tender, about 20 minutes. Add salt, pepper and a little more olive oil, again to taste.

Stir the bean purée and loosen with a little olive oil until it is very smooth. To serve, place a dollop of broad bean purée beside some radicchio on each plate, and eat warm!

SERVES 4

—1kg (2lb 4oz) *catalogna* chicory or, in season, 3 round heads of *radicchio*
—extra virgin olive oil
—2 garlic cloves, peeled and sliced
—a pinch of chilli flakes
—salt and freshly ground black pepper

BROAD BEAN PURÉE
—500g (1lb 2oz) split dried broad beans (fava beans)
—4 garlic cloves, skin on
—3 tablespoons extra virgin olive oil

*pulses*

# ZAMPONE E LENTICCHIE
*Pig's Trotter and Lentils*

*Zampone* (from *zampa*, pig's trotter) is a speciality of northern Italy. It is a boned pig's trotter stuffed with the gelatinous part of the trotter and pork meat. The trotter can be bought ready prepared and pre-cooked, in its own boiling bag. (You could also substitute the trotter with *cotechino*, a large pork sausage/ salami that needs to be cooked.)

Pigs' trotters are eaten traditionally by many Italians at New Year, usually, as here, with lentils (which represent money to come). A common accompaniment is *mostarda di Cremona*, which is fruit preserved in a syrup flavoured with mustard or horseradish.

Check the lentils for impurities such as little stones. Wash the lentils well.

Heat the olive oil in a large saucepan, then fry the garlic for a few minutes. Add the celery, tomatoes, washed lentils and the herbs, and cover with double its volume of water. Bring to the boil, then simmer for 30 minutes, adding a little more water if you think it necessary.

Meanwhile in another pan, cook the pre-cooked *zampone* in the bag in plenty of water for 20 minutes (it would be 3½ hours) cooking if you were using a raw trotter or a *cotechino*.

Drain the warm lentils if there is too much water, and season with salt and pepper to taste. Put the lentils on a serving plate, cut the sausage into slices and place on top of the lentils. Serve with the mustard fruits.

SERVES 4

- 200g (7oz) Castelluccio lentils
- 6 tablespoons extra virgin olive oil
- 2 garlic cloves, peeled and finely chopped
- 100g (3½oz) celery stalks, diced
- 100g (3½oz) sun-dried tomatoes, chopped
- a few fresh sage leaves
- 1 small sprig of fresh rosemary
- 1 *zampone* (pre-cooked pig's trotter), or *cotechino* sausage
- salt and freshly ground black pepper
- 1 x 450g (16oz) jar of mustard fruits (*mostarda di Cremona*), to serve

# POLENTA CONCIA
*Savoury Polenta*

Among quite a few recipes that remind me of Nina Burgai, a restaurateur in the Aosta Valley, this one stands out. As soon as you arrived at her hotel, 2,000 metres (6,500 feet) above sea level, hungry and tired, this polenta was the super-comfort food that she put on the table. It was invariably served with a chicken stew. She was also using her own ingredients, such as home-made butter and home-made Fontina cheese, making it so much more special.

This dish is good by itself, as a side dish to anything stewy, but it is also good when cold, cut into slices and fried.

Bring 1.5 litres (2¾ pints/6 cups) of water to the boil, add the salt, then slowly pour in the polenta, stirring all the time to avoid lumps. Cook and stir over a gentle heat for about 5–7 minutes (be careful of the splashes from the boiling polenta, which is very hot). After this time, the polenta will start to detach itself from the sides of the pan, which is the sign that it is cooked.

Now, add the butter and Fontina, then the Parmesan, and mix well. Stir everything together to a creamy texture, the cheeses and butter melting nicely.

Eat this hot as an accompaniment to stews of red meat, game, offal, vegetables, whatever you want. Or, if you have leftovers, leave to set in a flat dish, cut into slices and fry in some olive oil, or grill.

SERVES 6

—1 teaspoon salt
—300g (10½oz/1⅔ cups) instant polenta (instant cornmeal) (I am saving you about 40 minutes of stirring!)
—100g (3½oz) unsalted butter, cut into little cubes
—200g (7oz) Fontina cheese, cut into little cubes
—80g (2¾oz) Parmesan, freshly grated

*grains*

# BISCOTTI DI POLENTA
*Polenta Biscuits*

When I was a child I passed a bakery every day on my way to school in Borgo Franco. In the window they were always exhibiting their particular speciality, polenta biscuits. As I only knew polenta in a savoury context, these biscuits had a huge attraction for me, I was virtually in love with them! Some seventy years later I have learned to bake them for myself, and they are delicious.

Preheat the oven to 200°C (400°F/gas 6). Use a little extra butter to grease a couple of large baking trays.

Mix all the ingredients together in a bowl, including the butter, to a smooth mixture. Spoon the mixture into a piping bag and pipe small amounts – roughly 3cm (1¼ inches) in diameter – on to the buttered baking trays, leaving lots of space between as the biscuits will spread.

Put the baking tray into the preheated oven and bake the biscuits for 15 minutes. Remove from the oven and leave for a few minutes to cool. Using a cake slice, remove the biscuits to a wire rack. When cold, store them in an airtight jar for up to a year.

MAKES 30–40 BISCUITS

—150g (5½oz) unsalted butter, plus a little extra, softened
—300g (10½oz/1⅔ cups) very fine instant polenta (instant cornmeal)
—3 medium eggs, beaten
—finely grated zest of 1 lemon
—100g (3½oz/⅔ cup) Italian '00' flour, sifted
—1 teaspoon baking powder
—200g (7oz/1 cup) caster sugar (superfine sugar)

# PIZZOCCHERI DELLA VALTELLINA
*Buckwheat Pasta Bake*

Near Milan and bordering on Switzerland is the Valtellina, a charming valley that produces, among other things, good wine, the famous *bresaola* and the no less famous Bitto cheese. The latter, combined with buckwheat pasta (buckwheat grows well in this area), produces a very flavoursome baked pasta speciality.

Preheat the oven to 200°C (400°F/gas 6).

Cook the pasta in salted water together with the beans (or the other greens) and the diced potatoes until tender, about 15 minutes. Drain.

Layer some of the mixture in a large ovenproof dish, and sprinkle with the cubed cheese and Parmesan. Layer in this way again, until all the ingredients have been used.

In a pan, heat the butter until foaming. Add the nutmeg, sage and garlic, and pour over the vegetables in the dish. Bake in the preheated oven for 25 minutes. Mix with a serving spoon and serve.

SERVES 6

- 350g (12oz) *pizzoccheri* (buckwheat pasta)
- 200g (7oz) green beans, topped, tailed and halved, or spinach or Swiss chard, chopped
- 200g (7oz) potatoes, peeled and diced
- 250g (9oz) Bitto cheese, or Fontina or Taleggio, cubed
- 100g (3½oz) Parmesan, freshly grated
- 100g (3½oz) unsalted butter
- freshly grated nutmeg
- 10 fresh sage leaves, chopped
- 3 garlic cloves, peeled and finely sliced
- salt and freshly ground black pepper

# RISOTTO CON PORCINI
## *Wild Mushroom Risotto*

When people ask me what my favourite dish is, I have to say that this must be it. First I like rice and then I like mushrooms, especially the cep (*porcino* in Italian, the *Boletus edulis*). Not surprisingly, I prefer this risotto made with fresh *porcini*, but it is possible to make it with cultivated mushrooms, although it won't taste nearly so delicious…

It takes around 20 minutes to make a decent risotto. You should have a good stock simmering next to the pan in which the risotto is going to be made. This is important because the hot stock maintains the temperature of the rice while cooking, without any interruption.

Heat the olive oil and half the butter in a large shallow pan, and fry the onion for about 10 minutes, until softened a little.

Meanwhile, wipe the mushrooms, wild or cultivated, with a wet cloth, then cut them into slices. If using, slice the rehydrated dried *porcini* as well.

Add the rice and mushrooms to the onion pan and stir around to coat each rice grain with fat. Now start adding the hot stock in ladlefuls. Start to stir, and as soon as the first lot of liquid is absorbed, add some more, but not enough to drown it. Repeat for about 15 minutes – stirring and adding stock – which is when you should taste a grain of rice for your preferred *al dente* texture. Keep the rice moist but not too wet. Season to taste with salt and pepper.

Mix in the remaining butter and the grated Parmesan. Serve immediately.

SERVES 4

—1.5 litres (2³⁄4 pints / 6 cups) good stock (veal, chicken, beef or vegetable)
—3 tablespoons extra virgin olive oil
—60g (2¹⁄4oz) unsalted butter
—1 onion, peeled and finely chopped
—300g (10¹⁄2oz) fresh cep mushrooms, or 300g (10¹⁄2oz) field mushrooms and 20g (³⁄4oz) dried ceps (*funghi porcini*), softened in hot water for 20–30 minutes
—300g (10¹⁄2oz / 1¹⁄2 cups) *carnaroli* risotto rice
—salt and freshly ground black pepper
—60g (2¹⁄2oz) Parmesan, freshly grated

*grains*

# RISOTTO ALLA MILANESE CON OSSOBUCO
*Saffron Risotto with Veal Shin*

Of the many *risotti* that exist in the Po Valley, the Italian rice-growing area, *risotto milanese* is perhaps the most famous – and the most delicious. It has been so valued that one chef, wanting to celebrate it, covered it with a small square of gold leaf! I don't think this is entirely necessary, as the risotto is precious enough as it is, especially if you were able to use the *acquerello carnaroli* rice produced by my friends Piero and Marianava Rondolino (Livorno Ferraris/Piedmont).

Start with the veal shin. Dip the shin slices in flour and fry on each side in the olive oil in a large saucepan or braising pan. When golden, after about 5 minutes on each side, put on to a plate. In the same pan with the same oil, fry the onion, celery and carrot for about 5 minutes. Return the meat to the pan, add the wine and tomato purée, and stir together. Add the stock and rosemary, and braise until the meat detaches from the bone. This should take about 1½ hours. Season with salt and pepper to taste, and keep warm while you finish the risotto.

About 30 minutes before the veal is ready, start the risotto. Have the stock warming in a saucepan nearby. Using a large pan, fry the very finely chopped onion in half the butter until soft, about 10 minutes. Add the rice, and stir to ensure each grain is covered with fat. Now pour in the wine, and cook to let this evaporate for a couple of minutes. Add the saffron too, then start to add the simmering stock, ladle by ladle. Let each ladleful be absorbed before adding the next. Continue stirring and adding stock until the rice is *al dente* (some 15–20 minutes). Taste for salt and add if necessary.

Add the remaining butter and the grated Parmesan to the risotto. Stir very well, and serve with the *ossobuco*.

SERVES 4–6

- 4–6 *ossobuchi* (slices of veal shin on the bone, with bone marrow)
- plain flour (all-purpose flour), for dusting
- 6 tablespoons extra virgin olive oil
- 1 onion, peeled and finely chopped
- 3 celery stalks, finely chopped
- 1 carrot, finely chopped
- 100ml (3½fl oz/just under ½ cup) white wine
- 2 tablespoons tomato purée
- 200ml (7fl oz/just over ¾ cup) good beef or chicken stock
- 1 small sprig of fresh rosemary
- salt and freshly ground black pepper

RISOTTO
- 1.5–2 litres (2¾–3½ pints/6–8 cups) good beef or chicken stock
- 1 onion, peeled and very finely chopped
- 100g (3½ oz) unsalted butter
- 350g (12oz/1¾ cups) *carnaroli* risotto rice
- 100ml (3½fl oz/just under ½ cup) dry white wine
- ½ teaspoon powdered saffron or 10 saffron strands
- 60g (2¼oz) Parmesan, freshly grated

## RISOTTO CON LE SEPPIE
*Black Risotto with Cuttlefish*

It is always a bit traumatic for people not in the know to be confronted in a Venetian restaurant with this speciality – black rice with a delicate fishy taste. The little cuttlefish of the Venice *laguna* are laden with ink, which is what colours the rice (and is also used as drawing ink). In the Veneto, for this risotto they use an indigenous risotto rice, which has short and round grains, called *vialone nano*.

Prosecco is the famous sparkling wine of Venice, which is the perfect drink while sitting and looking at the bustle of the Grand Canal. However, most Venetians stir their glasses of Prosecco before drinking, which has the effect of getting rid of the bubbles! Heating Prosecco has exactly the same effect, so you could, of course, use white wine instead . . .

Get your fishmonger to clean the cuttlefish for you, if you can, but you must ask him to retain the ink sacs. Or, to do it yourself, pull the head and tentacles from the body tube. Take out the backbone and other internal matter. Among these body contents you will find a little blue-silver-coloured bag, which contains the ink. Save this. Remove the outer skin from the body tube. Cut away the eyes and the central mouth from the tentacles, and chop the rest – body and tentacles – into 1cm (½ inch) pieces.

Put the stock into a suitable pot on the stove, next to where you will make the risotto, and keep it warm.

—500g (1lb 2oz) cuttlefish, preferably small ones
—1.5 litres (2¾ pints / 6 cups) fish stock (cube allowed)
—2 tablespoons extra virgin olive oil
—30g (1oz) unsalted butter, plus a generous knob to finish
—1 small onion, peeled and finely chopped
—350g (12oz / 1¾ cups) *vialone nano* or other risotto rice
—75ml (2½fl oz / ⅜ cup) Prosecco
—salt and freshly ground black pepper

Heat the olive oil and butter in a large shallow pan, and fry the onion for about 10 minutes, until softened a little. Add the cuttlefish pieces, and fry for a further 10 minutes. Add the rice and stir around to coat each grain with fat. Pour in the Prosecco, and let it evaporate for a couple of minutes. Now start adding the hot stock in ladlefuls. Start to stir, and as soon as the first lot of liquid is absorbed, add some more, but not enough to drown it. Repeat for about 18–20 minutes – stirring and adding stock – which is when you should taste a grain of rice for your preferred *al dente* texture. Keep the rice moist but not too wet.

When you are happy with the texture of the rice, add the ink and the extra knob of butter. Season to taste with salt and pepper, then stir well and serve – but not, please, with cheese.

SERVES 4

*grains*

RISOTTO
CON LE
SEPPIE
*Black Risotto
with Cuttlefish
Pages 216–7*

# FREGOLA CON MOSCARDINI
*Sardinian Couscous with Baby Octopus*

Imagine the normal grains of couscous as eaten in Morocco. Then imagine giant grains about ten times the size. This is the Sardinian *fregola*, which is usually made by hand: a girl's ability to make *fregola* was once the benchmark for her suitability as a bride! *Fregola* is made of durum wheat semolina and is delicious. *Moscardini* are mini octopus, which can be found frozen – but they are obviously better fresh.

Heat the olive oil in a large pan and fry the garlic and chilli for 2 minutes. Add the tomato and wine, then simmer for about 5 minutes. Add the octopus and cook for another 7–8 minutes.

Meanwhile, cook the *fregola* in boiling salted water for 12 minutes. Drain and add to the sauce. Mix together well, taste for seasoning, then add the basil and serve. You don't need any cheese here . . .

SERVES 4

—150g (5¹/₂oz / ³/₄ cup) *fregola*
—small handful of fresh basil leaves
—salt and freshly ground black pepper

SAUCE
—6 tablespoons extra virgin olive oil
—1 garlic clove, peeled and finely chopped
—¹/₂ teaspoon chopped fresh red chilli
—1 ripe tomato, finely cubed
—50ml (2fl oz / ¹/₄ cup) dry white wine
—750g (1lb 10oz) baby octopus, cleaned

# PASTIERA DI GRANO
## *Neapolitan Easter Wheat Cake*

Grain, especially wheat, is a very important ingredient in Italy. Once upon a time, it was used as payment, and this 'wheat tart', has some religious significance as well. It is made at Easter in the south of Italy, especially in Naples, to give as a present.

Soak the grains in water to cover for 24 hours, changing the water occasionally. Drain, and pour the milk over the grains in a saucepan. Simmer with the lemon and orange zest for 45 minutes over a very low heat, until tender. (If using ready-prepared grains, you obviously don't need these first steps.) Add the cinnamon and vanilla now.

Meanwhile, make the pastry. Put the flour into a bowl, and mix in the butter or lard until the texture of breadcrumbs. Mix in the sugar, then the egg yolks, and stir with a wooden spoon – or your hands – until you have a smooth pastry. Wrap in clingfilm (plastic wrap) and chill in the refrigerator for 1½ hours.

Put the ricotta, egg yolks and orange-blossom water into a bowl. Add the candied peel and cooked grains and mix together. Beat the egg whites with the sugar until stiff and fold very gently into the filling, using a metal spoon.

Butter a large flan tin 35cm (14 inches) in diameter and 5cm (2 inches) deep. Preheat the oven to 190°C (375°F/gas 5). On a lightly floured surface, roll the chilled pastry out to a 5mm (¼ inch) thickness. Line the flan tin with the pastry. Cut off any surplus, which you will need for the lattice.

Pour the filling into the pastry case, and spread with a knife. Roll out the remaining pastry, cut into long strips and make a lattice pattern on the tart. Brush with the melted butter and bake for 45 minutes. Sprinkle with icing sugar before serving hot or cold.

SERVES 8–10 OR MORE

### PASTRY
—300g (10½oz/2¼ cups) plain flour (all-purpose flour)
—150g (5½oz) unsalted butter or lard, in small pieces
—150g (5½oz/1½ cups) caster sugar (superfine sugar)
—3 large egg yolks

### FILLING
—200g (7oz/1 cup) whole-wheat grains (sometimes sold as wheat berries), or 440g (14oz/about 2¾ cups) prepared wheat grains from an Italian deli
—500ml (18fl oz/2 cups) milk (if cooking your own wheat)
—finely grated zest of ½ a lemon and ½ an orange
—1 teaspoon ground cinnamon
—1 teaspoon vanilla extract
—300g (10½ oz/1½ cups) fresh ricotta cheese
—4 large eggs, separated
—50ml (2fl oz/¼ cup) orange-blossom water
—150g (5½oz) mixed candied peel, finely chopped
—225g (8oz/1 cup) caster sugar (superfine sugar)

### TO FINISH
—a little unsalted butter, melted
—icing sugar (confectioners' sugar)

*grains*

HERBS, SPICES
AND NUTS

Almost as important as the vegetables themselves are the additional flavourings we use to enhance particular vegetable dishes. Herbs and spices have been used in this way since the very earliest times, the former particularly in Italy. Most herbs and spices are plant-based – apart from salt, of course – which is why they are included here. It is commonly thought to be a myth that herbs and spices were used in medieval times to disguise the flavour of meat that was slightly off; but both also had ante-putrefactive properties, making that same meat safer to eat – as well, of course, as making it more interesting and palatable. For herbs and spices not only add taste, but their essential oils contribute to the digestibility of many foods. The rosemary and garlic served with lamb perform a dual purpose (as does the apple served with pork, or the orange juice with duck): they cut through and improve the digestibility of the fat. Herbs and spices are just as useful, in a flavouring and health sense, when used with vegetables.

Nuts are not vegetables, but they are used in significant ways in Italian cooking, and they too are plant-based.

# HERBS AND SPICES

Most of the culinary herbs we use are native to the Mediterranean, and it was the Ancient Romans who introduced many of them (and so many other things, such as garlic, onions, fruits like apples and cherries, and chestnuts) to the rest of Europe, including the cold north and Britain. Spices, on the other hand, play a lesser role in the cooking of Italy now, because most of them are exotic, coming from the tropics, rather than indigenous to the Mediterranean. They are usually the seeds of plants (like fennel), or the bark (cinnamon), pods (vanilla) or buds (cloves). They were as fashionable in the Middle Ages in Italy, as they were in Britain. I discovered this when I was trying to recreate a Bartholomeo Scappi dish (a sixteenth-century chef) for a television programme for the BBC. While it has been said that spices were added in England to hide the smell and taste of old meat, in Italy, especially in Rome, spices were added to make dishes more exotic for those high up in the Catholic Church (Scappi cooked for cardinals and popes in Rome). The *porchetta* (stuffed and roasted piglet) I cooked to remember those times included cinnamon, cloves, saffron, sugar, pepper, chilli, ginger and coriander, and not in small pinches either. Interestingly, some of these spices are still very much used and loved in Italian cooking, but they are used much more subtly.

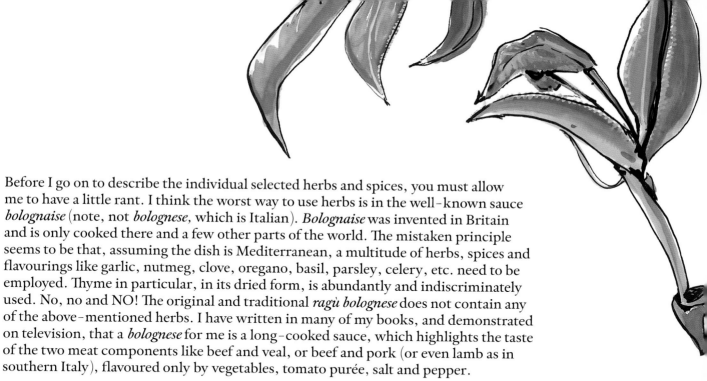

Before I go on to describe the individual selected herbs and spices, you must allow me to have a little rant. I think the worst way to use herbs is in the well-known sauce *bolognaise* (note, not *bolognese*, which is Italian). *Bolognaise* was invented in Britain and is only cooked there and a few other parts of the world. The mistaken principle seems to be that, assuming the dish is Mediterranean, a multitude of herbs, spices and flavourings like garlic, nutmeg, clove, oregano, basil, parsley, celery, etc. need to be employed. Thyme in particular, in its dried form, is abundantly and indiscriminately used. No, no and NO! The original and traditional *ragù bolognese* does not contain any of the above-mentioned herbs. I have written in many of my books, and demonstrated on television, that a *bolognese* for me is a long-cooked sauce, which highlights the taste of the two meat components like beef and veal, or beef and pork (or even lamb as in southern Italy), flavoured only by vegetables, tomato purée, salt and pepper.

My involvement with herbs came early. My mother, as did most people living in houses with balconies, used to keep a few terracotta pots containing fresh herbs to use in cooking and salads. Basil, rosemary, parsley and sage were the most usual, and many people kept a few tomato plants. When I was about six or seven, and living in the small railway flat near where my father was the stationmaster, I was in charge of collecting the peppery and flavoursome *rucola* (rocket, or arugula) for the daily salad. The *rucola* grew wild by the side of the railway tracks, so it didn't involve many food miles. Being so young, I was very proud to be doing something to contribute to the collective family pot.

**Aniseed** (*anice*) is a herbal plant from the same family as fennel and dill. The seeds have an intense flavour, which is used mostly in the drinks and confectionery industries. The Sardinians use aniseeds in sweet biscuits called *anicini*, and the anise-tasting seeds go very well with figs. They are also used in some savoury dishes, such as salads and fish.

His Majesty **basil** (*basilico*) is the herb I like the most. Very jokingly, I often say that I could make love on a bed of basil. But let's keep it in the kitchen, where His Majesty finds many ways of making dishes, salads and soups taste like heaven. The most important use of basil is in *pesto alla genovese*, the world-famous sauce in which basil is married with garlic, pine nuts, grated Parmesan and olive oil; this is used to flavour pasta, *gnocchi* and *minestrone*, and as a dip or an addition to *crostini*. Basil crowns many pizzas and salads – a *panzanella* bread salad in particular – and it lends its flavour to many tomato sauces.

Basil is native to India rather than the Mediterranean. The Romans introduced it to Europe, where it has become very familiar, and central to Italian cuisine. In Greece, they have a very small-leaved basil plant, which has a very strong aroma; they use it in cooking, but also keep it on the windowsill in a flowerpot to keep mosquitoes at bay. This basil is much hardier than the larger-leaved basil (there are several types, most of them developed in Italy), and therefore easier to grow in more northerly gardens.

The sweet **bay** or bay laurel (*alloro, lauro*) is an evergreen tree native to Asia, but now well established in Europe. The aromatic leaves are useful in the kitchen. I use a couple of leaves when making stock, and when boiling chestnuts, as the leaves are antibacterial (you will find bay leaves in packs of dried figs to keep insects at bay). Tie a bay leaf in with other herbs for an *aromi* (*bouquet garni*), and place a couple of leaves on the base and top of a pâté. Use fresh leaves if you can, as the flavour is stronger than dried.

**Capers** (*capperi*) are the buds of a plant thought to be native to the Mediterranean. In Italy, capers are primarily grown on the hot islands of Pantelleria and Lipari, south of Sicily. The flower buds are picked before they open, then cured in vinegar, brine or salt. I think the salted ones are best, but they need to be soaked in some water, and drained well, before use. The intense flavour of capers is used in many ways in Italian cooking, particularly in salads and sauces; add them towards the end of cooking, so that their pungency is undiminished. They are one of the primary ingredients of a classic tartare sauce, and add their piquancy to the tuna sauce for *vitello tonnato*.

If the caper buds are allowed to grow on and flower, the plant develops a fruit, which is pickled as the caper berry.

**Celery** (*sedano*) leaves – literally the leaves from the tops of a head of celery – are mostly used to flavour broth or consommé in a similar way to lovage (a herb which is easy to grow at home, but impossible to find in shops). But you could use both, minimally and chopped, in stuffings for ravioli or vegetables, etc. Make your own celery salt by drying the leaves, then grinding them with coarse salt; keep in an airtight jar.

**Chervil** (*cerfoglio*) is an extraordinarily delicate little herbal plant, with a leaf that looks like flat-leaf parsley. In Italy, in season throughout the summer, it is used for its sweet and subtle, slightly liquoricey taste. Add it to sauces, salads, to steamed vegetables, to gentle broths such as *stracciatella*, but always at the last moment. It is one of the French *fines herbes*.

**Chives** (*erba cipollina*) belong to the onion family (see page 98). They grow from tiny bulbs, and the edible, green, needle-like stalks are hollow, tasting like a cross between onion and garlic. The pretty purple flowers are edible as well. Finely chopped, chives are scattered on soups and salads to provide a delicate and light flavour. Chives are widely used, coarsely chopped, on salads, egg dishes and *crostini*.

**Cinnamon** (*cannella, cinnamomo*) is one of the most famous spices. It comes from the bark of an Asian tree, and has a strong, sweet flavour. It is used minimally in Italy, mostly in savoury dishes, adding richness to stews and sauces. It even features in a northern sausage risotto, revealing the influence of Venice, which was the main importer of eastern spices during the Middle Ages. Ground cinnamon is used as a flavouring for desserts as well, particularly in the Sicilian *cannoli*, and is occasionally sprinkled over fresh fruit.

**Coriander (cilantro)** (*coriandolo*) is relatively unknown in Italy, although it was familiar in the past. Now coriander is mostly associated with Chinese and Thai cooking and with some Middle Eastern cuisines. The leaves are used in cooking, to scatter at the end of cooking, or in salads. Coriander is a plant – like fennel – that produces both a herb, the leaves, and a spice, the seeds. Coriander seeds are, very curiously, sometimes used together with pistachios to flavour an Italian *salami* called *mortadella*. (Peppercorns are more common.) Coriander seeds are also used in syrups for liqueurs, and in the baking industry.

Coriander as a herb, and others like it, are reappearing in experimental cuisine in Italy, in an attempt to achieve new flavours. This can also involve *wasabi* from Japan, ginger, lemongrass and basil from Thailand, curry leaves or powder from India. However, it is not easy to use these herbs; in certain combinations only, they can fit very well with specific ingredients. The important thing is never to overdo it.

**Dill** (*aneto*) is another plant that produces both herb and spice. Because it closely resembles fennel (and is of the same botanical family), the Italians – who don't use dill much – call it *finocchio bastardo*. The herb leaves are mostly used in fish dishes in northern countries like Scandinavia; they are most famously used in the curing of fresh salmon, *gravadlax*, and in the cooking of traditional crayfish (*gamberi di fiume*). Dill seeds are often seen in recipes for pickled cucumbers or gherkins, as they are considered to be digestive (and are the main ingredient in the dill water given to colicky babies).

**Fennel** (*finocchio*) is yet another plant that produces both herb and spice (and a vegetable, developed in Italy, see page 27), all of which have a sweet anise flavour. The leaves are used elsewhere to flavour fish, but do not seem to be so popular in Italy. The seeds, however, are used in the south of Italy. A fennel flavour characterizes the liqueur Sambuca. Fennel seeds are also used in breads, in *taralli*, which are savoury biscuits based on olive oil, and in sweet biscuits. They find their way too into the *salami* industry, where they are used to flavour hot sausages, and particularly, *finocchiona*, a Tuscan speciality tasting of fennel.

*Finocchietto selvatico*, or wild fennel, is very special. It grows abundantly in Sicily, where it is used fresh, and is irreplaceable in the making of *pasta con le sarde*, a classic Palermo dish with sardines and wild fennel in the sauce (you can use fennel seeds instead). Naturally wild fennel, leaves and seeds, is also used for soups and for flavouring other vegetable dishes.

There are three types of **marjoram** (*maggiorana*): sweet or knotted marjoram, pot marjoram and wild marjoram or oregano (*origano*). They originated in Asia, but are now found all over Europe, both fresh and dried. Fresh they have a more delicate, minty scent; dried, the flavour is more intense. Marjoram is particularly popular in Liguria, where it is used in a stuffed breast of veal (*cima all genovese*) and in *preboggion*, a paste of green herbs used to fill a Ligurian ravioli called *pansôti*. Both, dried, are used as flavouring for pizza, for stuffings, and for sauces. Oregano, much more pungent than the other marjorams, is famous for its use in *pizzaiola*, a rich tomato sauce for beef. It is also used in biscuits, breads, and to flavour cured olives.

Of the various varieties of **mint** (*menta, mentuccia, nepitella*), peppermint is preferred in savoury dishes such as *zucchini alla scapece* (courgette very thinly sliced, then fried and marinated with oil, garlic, vinegar and mint). I use it too with roasted or grilled eel. Mint is good in salads, giving them a very refreshing fragrance. But I can't understand the British mixture of mint and vinegar as an accompaniment to lamb…

The only **parsley** (*prezzemolo*) used by Italians is the flat-leaf one, which has a better flavour than the curled version. It is the major ingredient in *salsa verde*, a green sauce (see page 239), and features in many fish and egg dishes, as well as being sprinkled on any number of finished dishes. As a result, there is a saying in Italy that someone who pops up everywhere, is omnipresent, is like parsley, '*essere come il prezzemolo*'!

**Peppercorns** (*pepe*) come in many colours – black, white, green and pink – and are the fruit of a vine native to India, Pakistan and Indonesia. Black and white peppercorns are used in Italy in stocks, and to season dishes and preserved products such as *salume* and hams. Always buy good peppercorns, buy them frequently, and only grind them just before use (or they will lose their essential oils).

**Rosemary** (*rosmarino*) is another typical Italian herb, which is used mostly with meat, especially roast meat. The fresh needles impart a very specific taste to chicken, veal, beef, lamb, game of any sort, but are used also in sauces – with the exception of *bolognese* sauce, where no herbs whatsoever are used. I use it with roast potatoes. Rosemary is cultivated, and you can happily grow it in a pot or in the garden; it can also be found growing wild on Italian hills and mountains – it is native to the Mediterranean – and is very similar in flavour and appearance to the cultivated one. One curious way with rosemary is putting some sprigs in a jar of sugar as you might vanilla, for a flavoured sugar.

**Saffron** (*zafferano*) is used very parsimoniously in Italian cooking, as it is so expensive. The spice comes from the dried stigmas of the saffron crocus, an Eastern crocus; these have to be picked by hand, and it takes the stigmas of some half a million flowers to make a kilo (couple of pounds) of spice! Most of the world's saffron is grown in Spain, but there are some plantations in Italy, most notably in Abruzzi and Sardinia. The most famous usage of saffron in Italian cooking is in the golden grains of a *risotto milanese* (which traditionally accompanies *ossobuco*), but it lends its colour and wonderful flavour to a few fish dishes as well. I once even invented a saffron ice cream…

**Sage** (*salvia*) is quite important in Italian cuisine. Fresh sage leaves are gently sautéed in butter for a simple sauce for *ravioli* or pan-fried veal liver; it is a major ingredient in veal *saltimbocca*, and it is also used in many stuffings mixed with other herbs (as it is in Britain). It is tender, so if grown in a pot it will need to be brought indoors in northern Europe.

**Salt** (*sale*) is probably the most commonly used flavour enhancer in all cooking. It is not vegetable based, but it has an important role in vegetable cooking (and indeed in all cooking). It was the earliest preserving agent used by man, and it is still used all over the world to preserve fish (such as cod, herrings and anchovies), meat (in the many Italian pork *salume*), and to preserve capers, a very characteristic Italian flavour. Salt was once so important that it was sold in special shops, and the word 'salary' in English comes from the Latin word for salt. Sea salt is produced mainly in Trapani, Sicily, and in parts of Sardinia, from salt pans in which seawater is evaporated by the sun, leaving the salt.

**Tarragon** (*dragoncello, estragone*) has become more popular in Italy in recent years. It is used in sauces to go with chicken, fish or eggs, and in salads or as a garnish. Combined with chopped garlic, tarragon turns *sauce hollandaise* into *sauce béarnaise*, which is eaten with steak or roasted fish. Tarragon should be used sparingly because it has quite a strong taste.

**Thyme** (*timo*) is hardier than marjoram, but not dissimilar in look and flavour – perhaps even a little more intense in flavour than marjoram. The little leaves can be used fresh – the easiest to find is the wild – but they can also be dried. Both are used in marinades, in sauces, soups, stuffings, stocks, in the liquid for cooking pulses, and lend their pungency to an *aromi* (*bouquet garni*). It is strong, so should be used sparingly.

## NUTS

Nuts are the fruits or seeds of certain plants, usually trees, and the inside of the hard shell is known as the kernel. Nuts in Italy are as important as fruit, and like fruit are eaten fresh, or dried to preserve them. Nuts are a concentrated food source, containing many nutrients such as protein. They are also very rich in oils, many of which are healthy to use in cooking – but must be bought in small quantities, as all nut oils go rancid very quickly. In Italy, nuts often take the major role in a recipe, while in some other cases they just play a participating role, but all are in one way or another quite important to the Italian economy.

The **almond** (*mandorla*) tree, related to the peach and apricot, is an ancient import from Central Asia and China: the trees were brought along the Silk Road into the Mediterranean, and naturalized happily in Spain and Italy. (They are now grown all over the world, particularly in Florida.) There are two basic varieties of almonds, sweet and bitter; seeds of the bitter almond contain traces of prussic acid, so the majority of almonds under cultivation around the world are sweet. In Italy, almonds are grown mainly in the Veneto, Puglia, Campania and in Sicily and Sardinia. The fruit is formed of an outer leathery skin, within which a hard shell forms, which encloses the seed, the almond itself.

In the Italian south, and in parts of the Middle East, almonds are eaten raw, when soft and green, before the internal hard shell develops. In Sicily, they also squeeze them at this stage to produce almond milk (*latte de mandorle*). When dry and minced they are

used with egg whites in the making of marzipan, *marzapane* (or *pasta reale*, as they call it in Sicily), to make sweets of all sorts, often formed into fruit shapes. Marzipan is used in Sicily to make *cassata*, as well as biscuits. *Torrone* (nougat) made with almonds (*torrone mandorlato*) is a great speciality (and you can also find *torrone* made with peanuts and hazelnuts). Ground almonds can replace flour in many cake recipes, and they are used in the making of *amaretti* biscuits: a proportion of bitter almonds – heat-treated to make them safe – are included to give that unique flavour. Almonds are also used to make an oil, which is used in cooking, medicine and beauty (it is an excellent base massage oil). Since Roman times, almond shells have been used to fire brick kilns (they are still used in biomass converters) and, finally, almonds lend their flavour to the famous liqueur, Amaretto.

As a child, there was a type of **chestnut** (*castagna*) I used to adore. These were sold near the sanctuary of Montevergine in Avellino, called *castagne del prete* or 'priest chestnuts'. They were cooked, semi-dried and put on strings to be sold or stored. The chestnut has been a great source of nourishment for thousands of years, especially for the population of the mountains of northern Italy and the Apennines. Probably originally from Asia, the sweet chestnut tree produces a fruit that is wrapped in a very prickly casing; a brown and shiny, firm peel encloses the nut, which also has a further skin adhering to it. Chestnuts are the only nuts to contain vitamin C, and they are also low in fat and rich in carbohydrate. The latter quality is one reason for their usefulness in areas of *cucina povera* (roughly the 'cooking of poverty'). A versatile fruit, the chestnut was and is eaten boiled or roasted from fresh – famously in the *caldallessa* or *ballotta*, a dish of freshly boiled chestnuts served with wine in northern Italian *trattorias*. They are also dried to preserve them; these can be ground to make chestnut flour, which is used for a kind of polenta porridge (useful before maize was introduced) and even pasta; *castagnaccio* is a cake made from chestnut flour and, when mixed with water, sugar and vanilla, chestnut flour makes *crema di castagne*, a filling for sweet ravioli. Regenerated, dried chestnuts are used in cooking quite a lot, in soups, in stuffings, as a vegetable, and chopped and whipped with cream in the famous dessert *montebianco*. Chestnuts can also be frozen after being peeled. I will never forget the chestnut jam my granny used to make with roasted chestnuts; this tasted just like *marroni canditi* (or *marrons glacés* as they are known in France). These are made in Italy from a particular chestnut variety called *marroni*; these chestnuts grow singly in their spiky skin, not in clusters like ordinary chestnuts.

If you roast your own chestnuts – rather than buy them from a stall – be sure to make an incision in the shiny skin first, so that they do not explode in the oven. You can buy special chestnut roasting pans, which have holes in the bottom; these can be put on the open fire, or on a barbecue.

The **hazelnut** (*nocciola, avellana*) comes from a tree native to the northern hemisphere. It is cultivated in both the south and north of Italy, principally in Campania, where the city of Avellino actually takes its name from its most famous crop. My granny used to live there, and had a small plantation of hazelnuts; in season, the crop was large enough to occupy one whole room of her house! I remember at festivals in autumn, hazelnuts were sold toasted, pierced and threaded on to pieces of string, resembling a necklace.

Like almonds, hazelnuts are used in *torrone* or nougat, but in Italy they are mainly combined with chocolate. The famous *gianduja* of Turin, a hazelnut and chocolate spread, was invented during Napoleonic times. When the city was under siege by the British, a *chocolatier* extended the little chocolate he had with some chopped hazelnuts, famously the variety La Tonda Gentile della Langhe. (This variety grows in the same region as the white Alba truffle, and the truffles from below hazelnut trees are reputed to be the best!) One of the most successful hazelnut and chocolate products, however, is Nutella, a modern version of *gianduja*, which has given Mr Ferrero of Alba great commercial success. A hazelnut oil is delicious used in salads, and a hazelnut liqueur is produced in Piedmont – Frangelico – which is sold in a bottle shaped like a monk in his habit. I love hazelnuts, and have developed some new recipes with them (see pages 120 and 248).

The monkey nut or **peanut** *(arachide)* is a member of the legume family, therefore botanically is a pulse rather than a nut. The peanut is also known as the groundnut because it buries its seed pods in the ground to ripen. It is a hugely important world crop, originating from South America, and is grown in Italy, primarily in Puglia and Campania. Peanuts find their way into biscuits and *torrone* (nougat), but their prime usage is as they do in the south of Italy, a very Arabic custom: they shell and eat roasted peanuts during the *passeggio*, the pre-dinner walk in the local *corso* (main street). (***Lupini*** or lupin seeds, **sunflower** seeds and **pumpkin** seeds are also eaten in the same way.) Groundnut oil is a familiar item in many kitchens: it has a high smoke point, so can be used in frying, unlike other nut oils.

Stone pine trees, from which **pine kernels** or **pine nuts** (*pinoli*) come, are very much part of the Italian landscape. Their pine cones, on maturing, hold two nuts/seeds under each scale of the cone. In America, pine nuts are harvested by Native Americans; the pine kernels which come from Korean pines are much larger than the European or American. Pine nuts have been used as a food for thousands of years wherever pine trees grow; in Italy they are used in *tortes* and cakes, in stuffing for roasts, to enrich salads and, most famously, as a major ingredient of the famous Ligurian *pesto* sauce.

**Pistachio** (*pistacchio*) nuts are grown in Italy, with the best quality cultivated near to Mount Etna – more precisely Bronte, where Admiral Nelson stayed while in Sicily. The tree is typical of the southern Mediterranean. The most curious use of pistachio is in the *mortadella salame* from Bologna: it doesn't give much flavour, but adds visual appeal when sliced. Pistachios are eaten shelled as a snack – on the *passeggio*, like peanuts – and are also used in cakes, biscuits, *torrone*, sauces and as flavouring and colouring for a delicious Italian ice cream. Pistachio oil has a very strong flavour, and should be used to add flavour to foods, or in dressings.

Lastly the **walnut** (*noce*). The tree comes originally from Asia, and was introduced to Europe in around the fifteenth century. It is another quintessential nut used in Italy, and the best come from the Sorrento area in Campania. The fruits of the tree grow in clusters: a green outer shell encloses the brown, crinkly shell that hardens during the ripening process; this encloses the brain-like kernel. I adore 'green' walnuts, which you can peel while still fresh and tender (before the shell hardens), and which I eat with bread. (This is what is pickled in Britain.) I make *nocino* (see page 253) a digestive liqueur, every year with green walnuts. Every Italian region has a *nocino* but perhaps Emilia-Romagna is the main place, as *nocino* is a speciality of Modena. Walnuts that have been allowed to mature and dry are appreciated for their wrinkly kernels. These are sold in the shell, or shelled, and are used for sauces, the most important being the Ligurian *tocco de noce* to dress the herb-stuffed ravioli known as *pansôti al preboggion*. Walnuts can be used in cakes, *torte* fillings or simply eaten as they are. I also make *mostarda* every year, which is a heavenly tasting jam, cooked for 12 hours, combining fresh juice, apples, peaches, pears, plums, berries and walnuts. Walnut oil is delicious used in dressings.

## PESTO ALLA GENOVESE
### *Ligurian Basil Sauce*

The word '*pesto*' is closely connected to Genoa in Liguria (and vice versa!). This pasta sauce, consisting primarily of basil, is famous all over the world, and now also gives its name to sauces which are similar, but do not contain basil at all. In Liguria there are two versions of the sauce: one containing junket, which makes it milder, and the other simply oil. Pesto can also be used as a spread for *crostini* and *bruschetta*; it can be used with *gnocchi* instead of pasta; and you can also add a spoonful to a soup like *minestrone* for additional flavour.

Surplus home-made pesto can be frozen in ice-cube trays for future use.

Put the basil leaves, garlic and the sea salt, which will serve as a grinder, into a large mortar. Work the pestle to reduce the ingredients to a pulp. Add the pine nuts, which will give a delicate resinous taste, and continue to pound to a fine pulp.

Now add the Parmesan and, still continuing to pound, add enough olive oil to obtain a smooth sauce.

SERVES 4

—100g (3½oz) fresh basil leaves
—2 garlic cloves, peeled and chopped
—about 5–10g (⅛–¼oz) coarse sea salt
—40g (1½oz) pine nuts
—40g (1½oz) Parmesan, freshly grated
—100ml (3½fl oz / just under ½ cup) extra virgin olive oil, or as required

## ACCIUGHE CON SALSA VERDE
### *Anchovies with Green Herb Sauce*

This green sauce from Piedmont is based on parsley, and is used primarily in two ways: it accompanies *bollito misto* (mixed boiled meats) and anchovy fillets. The recipe below makes a batch that you can keep in the refrigerator for a couple of days. Serve as a starter with good bread, or as part of an *antipasto*.

Chop the parsley and garlic together extremely finely. Chop the pickled gherkins and chilli together, again very finely. Mix these ingredients together in a bowl.

Put some white wine vinegar into another bowl, add the breadcrumbs, and leave to soak for a few minutes. Squeeze the moisture out, then add the soaked breadcrumbs to the parsley mixture. Add just enough extra virgin olive oil to emulsify and make a thick sauce. Mix well.

Place a layer of anchovies at the bottom of a small porcelain dish. Top with a layer of *salsa verde* and continue until you finish with a layer of anchovies.

**MAKES ABOUT 450G (1LB)**

—300g (10½oz) good anchovy fillets in olive oil, drained

**GREEN HERB SAUCE**
—400g (14oz) fresh flat-leaf parsley leaves
—2 garlic cloves, peeled
—2 pickled gherkins
—1 small hot chilli, finely chopped
—a little white wine vinegar
—50g (1¾oz/1 cup) fresh white breadcrumbs
—extra virgin olive oil

*herbs*

**239**

# ZUCCHINI ALLA SCAPECE
*Pickled Fried Courgettes*

The word *scapece* most probably comes from *escabeche*, a Spanish word used for ingredients that are marinated. The Neapolitans especially love these almost burned slices of courgette (zucchini): they use them to accompany barbecued meats, but also like them for *antipasto*.

Cut the courgettes into 5mm (¼ inch) rounds.

Heat the olive oil in a large frying pan and shallow-fry the courgette slices until brown and soft. Arrange on absorbent kitchen paper to remove the excess oil.

Put the courgette slices into a serving bowl. Dress with the garlic, extra virgin olive oil, vinegar, and some salt and pepper to taste. Scatter over the mint leaves.

SERVES 4

—500g (1lb 2oz) small courgettes
  (zucchini), topped and tailed
—olive oil, for shallow-frying
—2 garlic cloves, peeled and
  finely sliced
—1½ tablespoons extra virgin olive oil
—1 teaspoon white wine vinegar
—1 small bunch of fresh mint leaves,
  finely chopped (about 2 tablespoons)
—salt and freshly ground black pepper

# NODINO DI VITELLO, BURRO E SALVIA
## *Veal Cutlet with Butter and Sage*

I have never known why it is called *nodino*, 'little knot'. A *nodino* is usually a thinnish cutlet with a bone, taken from the ribs, but not the one with the fillet, which is quite thick. The cut of veal, and the recipe, are very characteristic of the north of Italy, particularly Piedmont. You only want butter and sage for flavour, no garlic, nothing else; it's a very simple dish.

Dip the cutlets into the flour which you have seasoned with a little salt and pepper.

Melt the butter in a large frying pan, and add the cutlets and the sage leaves. Cook slowly, not too fast, until brownish on the outside and cooked inside, but not too well done, about 10–15 minutes.

Remove the cutlets from the pan, and serve with the browned sage butter over the top. Serve with boiled, fried or mashed potatoes, with perhaps some spinach.

SERVES 4

—4 veal cutlets, 250g (9oz) each, with bone
—a little plain flour (all-purpose flour), for dusting
—50g (1¾oz) unsalted butter
—2 tablespoons fresh sage leaves
—salt and freshly ground black pepper

*herbs*

# MERLUZZO CURATO ALL'ANETO
*Cod Marinated with Dill*

Dill, or *aneto* as they call it in Italy, used to be more common in Italian cookery a couple of centuries ago, and has now started to be popular again. The Swedish *gravadlax* is a prime example of how to marinate a fish to be eaten cured. Cod is used here, instead of salmon: the taste is very clean and fresh, making it an excellent starter.

Ask the fishmonger to take the skin off the piece of cod, and to remove any bones.

Put half the salt, half the sugar and half the dill into the base of a ceramic or steel container big enough to hold the piece of cod. Mix the mustard and horseradish (if using) together and spread on both sides of the fish, with plenty of ground black pepper. Put the fish into the dish, and cover with the remaining salt, sugar and dill. Cover the fish with foil and keep in the refrigerator for 2 days.

Serve thin slices of the cod with some sliced boiled potatoes or with toast.

SERVES 4

—500g (1lb 2oz) fresh cod, in the piece, filleted
—60g (2¼oz / just under ¼ cup) salt
—60g (2¼oz / ¼ cup) golden caster sugar (superfine sugar)
—2 bunches of fresh dill, finely chopped
—2 teaspoons English mustard
—1 tablespoon freshly grated horseradish (optional)
—1 tablespoon coarsely ground black pepper

# SALSICCIE FATTE A MANO CON FINOCCHIO
*Home-made Sausages with Fennel*

Italian sausages are in a league of their own. I am thinking of those from Norcia, the town in Umbria famous for its pork and wild boar products, and the wonderful fresh pork lucanica sausages. Here I am making my own sausages from pork meat, and flavouring them with fennel seeds – a traditional combination in the finocchio salame of Tuscany. You can, however, make the sausages with any other meat – wild boar, lamb, beef, veal, chicken or turkey – and you can spice them as you please – any other seeds, or something like fresh sage would be good.

Serve the sausages with polenta, or mashed potatoes. They could be served with pasta as well. A sauce made from peppers, or tomatoes or indeed a salsa verde would be a good accompaniment.

Put the pork, chilli, garlic, fennel seeds and wine into a bowl, and season with salt and pepper to taste. Mix well together, then, using your hands, divide into twelve pieces. Roll each piece into a sausage shape.

Heat 4–5 tablespoons of olive oil in a frying pan, and fry the sausages over a medium heat until they are golden on all sides. This will take about 10 minutes.

SERVES 6

- 1kg (2lb 4oz) minced pork
- 1 teaspoon chopped red chilli
- 2 garlic cloves, peeled and crushed
- 1 teaspoon fennel seeds
- 100ml (3$\frac{1}{2}$fl oz / just under $\frac{1}{2}$ cup) red wine
- salt and freshly ground black pepper
- extra virgin olive oil

*herbs*

**245**

# MARZAPANE FRESCO
*Fresh Marzipan*

There is an incredible difference between the commercial marzipan, and marzipan you have made at home yourself. The latter tastes infinitely more exciting and delicious. Should you want a stronger almond taste, use a few apricot kernels (available online or in Asian supermarkets) or some liquid almond extract.

In parts of the south of Italy, marzipan is called *pasta reale*, or 'royal paste', which shows how valued it is. In Sicily, for instance, they model fruit with marzipan, and paint it in realistic colours. You can make little biscuit shapes, of animals, people, etc. – and bake them in a hot oven for about 15 minutes. The inside will still be soft after this time. Or use the marzipan to wrap a mixture of ricotta, fruit and sponge to make a cake, known as *cassata* in Sicily.

Put the almonds into a bowl and pour enough boiling water over to cover them. Leave for 5 minutes. Drain and skin the almonds, one by one. This is boring, but needs to be done.

Mince the almonds coarsely, in a blender. You don't want too fine a texture. Mix with the sugar and carefully fold in the beaten egg whites. Work gently, until you obtain a paste.

Set aside to cool, and store in the refrigerator for a day at most.

MAKES 1.5KG (3LB 5OZ)

—1kg (2lb 4oz) shelled almonds, in their skins
—400g (14oz/4 cups) icing sugar (confectioners' sugar), plus extra for dusting
—4 medium egg whites, beaten until stiff

# MARMELLATA DI CASTAGNE
*Chestnut Jam*

My granny used to make this jam every autumn, and keep it under lock and key, away from the depredations of us children. It was so delicious, we couldn't resist it, as it tasted almost like minced *marrons glacés*. The jam didn't have any special function, apart from being eaten, by the spoonful, from the jar. It is not something to spread on bread, as the texture is too floury. It could be the filling for a sweet ravioli, that would be fried, not boiled – you could use shortcrust pastry as well as pasta dough. And, if you liked, you could serve a mound of jam with some whipped double cream: it's not very Italian, but it's delicious none the less!

—salt
—1.25kg (2lb 12oz) large fresh chestnuts
—2 fresh bay leaves
—1 vanilla pod (vanilla bean)
—1.25kg (2lb 12oz/6¼ cups) caster sugar (superfine sugar)

Bring a large saucepan of lightly salted water to the boil, and add the chestnuts, along with the bay leaves. Simmer for 30 minutes. Drain, and leave to cool.

Remove all the shells from the chestnuts, and as much inner skin as possible. This is fiddly, but needs to be done. Mince the chestnuts in a food processor, then pass through a sieve, to make a very fine and dry purée.

Slit the vanilla pod down the side, and scrape the seeds into a medium pan. Add the pod, the sugar and 200ml (7fl oz/just under 1 cup) of water, and place over a medium heat. Reduce this at a simmer to a syrup, which will take about 20 minutes.

Discard the vanilla pod, then add the chestnut purée to the syrup. Cook gently, stirring occasionally, for about 30 minutes.

Pour into sterilized jars (see page 143), and store for up to a month.

MAKES 2KG (4LB 8OZ)

# CROCCANTE DI NOCCIOLE E PISTACCHI
*Hazelnut and Pistachio Crunch*

This is perhaps the favourite Italian way of using hazelnuts, in a celebratory sweet that makes its appearance towards Christmas, and at *festas* from north to south. It can be made with almonds as well, or a mixture, as here. Eat as a sweet after a meal – or whenever you like!

Line two baking sheets with rice paper.

Put the sugar and honey into a large, heavy-based saucepan, and melt together gently. When melted, raise the heat slightly and cook until the sugar turns a light brown in colour. Add the orange zest and stir for a minute with a wooden spoon. Add the hazelnuts and pistachios, and stir together until the nuts are coated with syrup.

Pour this mixture on to the paper-lined baking sheets, and use the lemon halves as spatulas to spread the mixture out to about 2.5cm (1 inch) in thickness. (The lemons will not stick, unlike a wooden or plastic spatula.)

While still warm, cut the sticky mixture into whatever shapes you like – cubes of about 4cm (1½ inches) square are best. When completely cold, break the *croccante* into pieces, and store in an airtight jar.

MAKES 1KG (2LB 4OZ)

—2–3 sheets of rice paper
—400g (14oz/2 cups) golden caster sugar (superfine sugar)
—100g (3½oz) runny honey
—finely grated zest of 1 orange
—250g (9oz) shelled hazelnuts
—250g (9oz) shelled pistachio nuts
—1 lemon, halved

# TOCCO (SALSA) DI NOCE
*Ligurian Walnut Sauce*

This sauce is very typical of Liguria, where it is called *tocco di noxe*, and various *ravioli* are flavoured with it, especially those made with the herbs from the hills around Liguria. The sauce can also be used for other things, for little *tartines*, for other pasta such as *tagliatelle*, and can also be added to pesto. Add Parmesan, of course, if using as a pasta sauce.

You should strain the yoghurt to get most of the liquid out, which will give you a thicker end result.

Use a mortar and pestle to pound all the dry ingredients to a paste. Or you could use a food processor to blend.

Add the strained yoghurt gradually, mixing well, then season to taste. Dilute with a little olive oil, as required. You want a smooth, fairly thick, sauce.

Keep in the refrigerator for a couple of days only.

SERVES 4–5

—180g (6oz) shelled walnuts, blanched and skinned
—2–3 tablespoons fresh white breadcrumbs
—1 garlic clove, peeled and finely chopped
—1 teaspoon fresh thyme leaves
—4 tablespoons strained Greek yoghurt
—2 tablespoons extra virgin olive oil
—salt and freshly ground black pepper

*nuts*

# NOCINO O NOCILLO
## *Walnut Liqueur*

Depending whether you are in Modena (Emilia-Romagna) or in Naples (Campania and the Amalfi coast), you will find this mighty digestive offered at the end of a meal, especially during festivities. To make it properly, you must use green walnuts, which are not fully formed. These need to be picked on 23 June, the day of San Giovanni, when they say that the witches are particularly benevolent . . .

The alcohol will be difficult to get hold of in some countries. In the UK, try to convince your pharmacist that you need this alcohol, but it must be the edible variety. Or, do as I do, and buy it abroad, and bring it back in your car…

—1.5kg (3lb 5oz) green walnuts, picked before the nut inside is formed, quartered
—1.5 litres (2¾ pints/6 cups) pure spirit alcohol (95%)
—1 teaspoon freshly grated nutmeg
—1 teaspoon ground cloves
—1 cinnamon stick
—500g (1lb 2oz/2½ cups) caster sugar (superfine sugar)
—1 litre (1¾ pints/4 cups) water, warmed

Place the walnuts, alcohol and spices in a suitable glass container. (The nutmeg, cloves and cinnamon can be adjusted to your taste and pleasure.) Cover tightly with a lid, and leave to marinate, possibly in a sunny place, for 40 days. After this time the alcohol will have assumed a very dark brown to black colour.

Strain the liquid from the nuts, and discard the nuts.

Stir the sugar into the warm water in a pan or jug and dissolve. When cool, add this to the walnut liquid. Mix well and bottle (in thoroughly sterilized bottles, see page 143). This should result in an alcohol content of about 50–60 per cent. Should you prefer it weaker, add more water.

Serve in very small glasses after a special meal, and drink a little whenever you feel a bit down.

**MAKES ABOUT 2 LITRES (3½ PINTS)**

*nuts*

**253**

## PAN SPEZIATO (PANPEPATO)
### *Peppered Bread*

This bread is very reminiscent of the Middle Ages in Tuscany, when spices, imported from the Mediterranean, were used in profusion to produce savoury and sweet dishes. It is similar in concept to *panforte*, but is darker in colour because of the cocoa. It is also known in Umbria as *panpepato* because of its spiciness!

Put the raisins into a small bowl, and cover them with the Vin Santo. Leave to soak for 30 minutes.

Preheat the oven to 160°C (325°F/gas 3). Use the butter to grease a baking tray.

Mix all the ingredients together in a bowl, including the raisins and their soaking liquid. Add enough flour to obtain a fairly stiff, but not too stiff, mixture.

Shape with wet hands into two round loaves, and place them on a buttered baking tray. Bake in the preheated oven for 30 minutes, then leave to cool on a wire rack.

Serve in wedges, with coffee, or with liqueurs or dessert wine after a meal. In Italy, we tend to indulge in fruit and sweet things after a meal, so this would be perfect.

MAKES I LOAF, TO SERVE 6–8

—50g (1³⁄₄oz) Muscat raisins
—2–3 tablespoons Vin Santo
—a little unsalted butter, for greasing
—80g (2³⁄₄oz) blanched almonds, skinned and toasted
—80g (2³⁄₄oz) shelled hazelnuts, blanched and skinned
—80g (2³⁄₄oz) shelled walnuts, blanched and skinned
—50g (1³⁄₄oz) pine nuts
—80g (2³⁄₄oz) bitter cocoa powder
—100g (3¹⁄₂oz) candied peel, finely diced
—¹⁄₂ teaspoon each of ground cinnamon, ground coriander and freshly grated nutmeg
—1 tablespoon freshly ground black pepper
—180g (6oz) runny honey
—30g (1oz) plain flour (all-purpose flour)

TO FINISH
—plain flour (all-purpose flour), as required
—a little unsalted butter, for greasing

# GELATO DI PISTACCHIO
## *Pistachio Ice Cream*

The Doges of Venice were responsible for quite a few of the spices introduced into Italy, the result of their trade in all corners of the Mediterranean. This ice cream, made with pistachio nuts, is flavoured with cardamom, not a usual flavouring now in Italy, but at one time very popular.

Bring the milk to the boil, add the cardamom, then simmer for 5–10 minutes. Allow to cool, then strain.

In a separate bowl, mix the egg yolks, honey and sugar until creamy. Add the flavoured milk, a little at a time, and whisk in until the milk is used up. Place the mixture in a bain-marie or double boiler and cook gently for 15 minutes. (You could use a heatproof bowl set over a pan of boiling water, making sure the water is not touching the bowl.) Keep stirring to avoid lumps. Cover with clingfilm and leave to rest in the refrigerator overnight.

The next day, churn the mixture in an ice-cream machine for about 30 minutes.

Meanwhile, in a blender, reduce the pistachios to a fine cream. In a bowl, half whip the double cream: you want it still soft. Add the pistachio cream, whipped cream and green food colouring to the ice-cream machine in the last 5 minutes of churning. The ice-cream is ready. (If you don't have a machine, put the ice-cream mix into a container in the freezer for about an hour, then beat it with a fork and return it to the freezer. Do this two or three times. The last time you do this, add the cream, nuts and food colouring, then leave to freeze until firm.)

Serve in little bowls with chopped pistachios sprinkled over the top. Very nice with polenta biscuits (see page 208).

SERVES 6

- —500ml (18fl oz / 2 cups) full-fat milk
- —1 tablespoon ground cardamom
- —5 medium egg yolks
- —50g (1³/₄oz) runny honey
- —150g (5¹/₂oz / ³/₄ cup) caster sugar (superfine sugar)
- —100g (3¹/₂oz) shelled pistachio nuts, plus extra, chopped, to decorate
- —150ml (5fl oz / ²/₃ cup) double cream (heavy cream)
- —a touch of green food colouring

# MUSHROOMS AND TRUFFLES

I have already written two books on my favourite subject – my beloved fungi, or edible mushrooms and truffles – and hope that here, on a much smaller canvas, I will be able to introduce you to at least some ideas about such a vast field. For, you may be surprised to learn, there are at least some 200,000 different fungi, and mycologists – experts in the subject – are still discovering new varieties every year. The mycological world is absolutely enormous.

Fungi are not like other plants in that they do not 'feed' from the sun; they contain no chlorophyll, the green pigments that synthesize carbon compounds from the sun's energy. Instead fungi collect their nutrients entirely from living organisms, or from decaying or dead organic matter. In fact, without them we could not properly exist, for it is the task of many fungi to bring back to nature what was given by nature. They perform a vital role in breaking down dead matter, assisting in that matter's decomposition, and as a result of this valuable cleaning-up operation, fungi make further nourishment for the soil, creating a habitat for new generations of fungi and other plants. Other fungi affect our food: wines and beers are made through the interaction of fungi and sugar; breads rise because of the fungus that is yeast; and milk transforms into yoghurt because of fungal activity. There are also, of course, fungi whose role is less pleasant. Some fungi attack living trees or plants, killing them: Dutch elm disease, for instance, is caused by a microscopic fungus carried by certain beetles.

What we are interested in here, though, are the fungi which have fruiting bodies, the part which we can collect or buy, cook and eat. Most of you will be buying your mushrooms from shops and supermarkets, and the number of types available is constantly growing. Science and industry have managed to isolate the spores (seeds) of a few wild varieties, and now successfully cultivate them in large quantities. Some of you may, like me, be lucky enough to enjoy the 'quiet hunt', to be able to go into woods throughout Europe – and indeed further afield – and seek out wild fungi in their natural and, often, secret habitats. Looking for wild fungi is one of my greatest pleasures – followed closely by eating fungi! Not surprisingly, for me the flavour of the wild is always superior to the cultivated.

Never peel mushrooms, whether wild or cultivated. It is an old-fashioned way to treat them, and anyway it is the skin that contains the taste. If you find them a little dirty, just brush them with a soft brush. If you can avoid it, don't wash mushrooms either, as they absorb an enormous quantity of water, rendering them soggy and tasteless. A wipe with a damp cloth is all that is probably needed.

# CULTIVATED MUSHROOMS

Obviously all mushrooms were once available only from the wild, but it was in the Far East that a few were cultivated, possibly as early as 600 AD. Those first cultivated mushrooms were varieties you can still find mostly in the Far East today: among them *Auricularia polytricha* (wood ear), *Flammulina velutipes* (enoki) and *Lentinula edodes* (shiitake). **Wood ears** grow in cultivation on rotting wood; they are usually dried, but are easy to rehydrate. The Chinese use them a lot, for food and medicine. **Enoki** are tiny white mushrooms, grown and bought in clumps; they are so pretty, I like to use them raw, in salads and in soups, for both flavour and decoration. **Shiitake** are perhaps the most familiar of the 'exotic' mushrooms from the East; they are similar in shape and look like the cep or pennybun, but taste nothing like them. They are highly valued in Japan and China, and can be found fresh or dried.

Other Eastern cultivated mushrooms which are always available include the **oyster** (*pleuroto, gelone, fungo ostrica*) mushroom. There are four types of *Pleurotus*, which means mushrooms that grow 'sideways'. *P. ostreatus* (referring to the oyster-shaped cap) is the most familiar (it was cultivated in Germany during World War I as a subsistence food). In the wild the mushrooms grow on stumps of rotting trees, and come in various colours such as yellow and even pink; in cultivation they are grown in special composts. The latest addition to the *Pleurotus* family is the **imperial** or **king oyster** (*P. eryngii*), which is derived from the wild *cardoncello* mushroom growing in Puglia in Italy. This mushroom grows quite fleshy and large, and it is possible to cut it into slices: I prefer it dipped in flour, egg and breadcrumbs and fried. It can also be used in vegetable dishes like *lasagna* or timbales.

The Japanese and Chinese use a great deal of the above (and other) mushrooms in their cuisine, and have developed a very large industry to produce them. The finest mushroom of all for the Japanese, though, certainly as regards texture, is the **matsutake** (*Tricholoma matsutake*). This mushroom grows

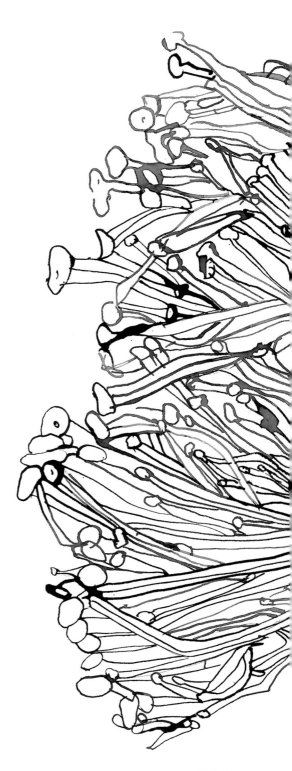

rather like a truffle, in symbiosis with the roots of certain trees, rather than feeding off dead or decaying matter. It is very difficult to cultivate, as a result, which means the mushroom is not readily available, thus it can command prices of around £500–£800 per kilogram ($350–$500 per pound)!

These Eastern specimens above are the more exotic varieties of cultivated mushroom, but we must not forget the more common and familiar western varieties. *Agaricus bisporus* is a cultivated relation of the wild field mushroom (*A. campestris*), and it has taken over the world! It has been cultivated from around the 1600s in Europe, most notably in caves near Bath in England, and in caves near Paris in France. So many were produced in Paris that small mushrooms are still to this day called *champignons de Paris*. There are various sizes. The smallest is the **button mushroom** or **champignon**, with a small white cap (when the cap is brown, it is known as **Paris brown**); **cap mushrooms** are slightly larger (and if brown on top are known as chestnut mushrooms); **flat or open mushrooms** have a totally developed, opened-out cap with visible brown gills. These mushrooms are very versatile, and are mostly used either fried in breadcrumbs, or steamed or grilled, or chopped and used for sauces. The **Portobello mushroom**, which has an open wide cap, is an invention of the trade because it is nothing other than *A. bisporus* which has been allowed to mature and grow quite large. These are usually grilled or stuffed and fried or baked.

# WILD MUSHROOMS

The first thing to say about wild mushrooms is that you must always be sure of what you are looking for and picking. If you are not a mycologist yourself, the surest safeguard – for many mushrooms are deadly poisonous – is to consult a professional, or to go on a fungus foray led by a professional. And always be careful not to deplete a mushroom site: cut the mushrooms carefully, rather than pulling them out of the ground, leaving the mycelium (the underground network which is the basis of fruiting bodies) as intact as possible.

The **field mushroom** (*Agaricus campestris*, or *prataiolo* in Italian), to which our common or garden button mushrooms are related, used to be much more available. With the loss of horse-drawn carriages and carts, though, fields lack the horse manure that these mushrooms like. But they are still to be found, as is their close relative, the horse mushroom (*A. arvensis*). You won't be able to buy these, but you can, in special

grocers, find **ceps** (*Boletus edulis*), **chanterelles** (*Cantherellus cibarius*) and **morels** (*Morchella elata*), collected wild in their seasons, because these three mushrooms cannot be cultivated.

The **cep** is my favourite wild mushroom, known to the Italians as *porcino* (little pig), and to the British as pennybun (the cap looks like a round bun with a shiny, sugar-baked top). The flavour is wonderful and I use them in a number of ways: raw in thin slices with a simple dressing, fried, baked, preserved, and they can be successfully dried. These dried *funghi porcini* are invaluable: after softening in hot water and chopping them, I use them to intensify the flavour of a dish using ordinary fresh mushrooms – such as a mushroom risotto or *tagliatelle con funghi*. The water should be used too, as it is full of flavour. (The leading stock-cube company in Italy, Star, has developed a stock cube with *porcini,* which gives a good taste of the wild mushroom. These are available internationally now.)

The **chanterelle** (*cantarello*) grows widely throughout Europe, and in North America. When I ran a restaurant, I used to get mine from Scotland. These are perhaps the prettiest mushrooms, like bright yellow frilled trumpets, and they often smell of apricots. Known to the French as both *chanterelles* and *girolles*, their colour, flavour and texture are wonderful in many dishes. **Morels** (*spugnola, gialla, elata*) are the first mushrooms to appear each year, in springtime (rather than in autumn). They are unusual to look at, with a sponge-like conical (rather than round) cap, and grow throughout Europe, in America and in northern Asia. I once bought 120 kilograms (265 pounds) of dried morels in Nepal! They can be cooked fresh, obviously, but are very successfully dried, and reconstitute well.

Three other wild mushrooms which you might encounter, and which are delicious to eat, are **Caesar's mushroom** (*Amanita caesarea*, or *ovolo* in Italian), **honey fungus** (*Armillaria mellea*, or *chiodino, famigliola buona*), and **horn of plenty** (*Craterellus cornucopioides*, or *trombetta dei morti, craterello*). I give recipes for their usage, and you may be lucky enough to find them, but if not, substitute any mushroom you have to hand.

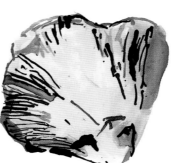

# TRUFFLES

Truffles, the kings of the fungi world, have fruiting bodies that develop only underground, and only in association with certain trees. This is why they are very difficult – or impossible – to cultivate, which dictates their rarity and thus their high price! Hundreds of truffle-like tubers grow around the world – from China to California – but only three possess the flavour and aroma that have ensured their primacy in the fungi world.

The best of all truffles is the **white truffle** (*Tuber magnatum*, or *tartufo bianco* in Italian) which grows only in Italy. Most come from Piedmont, around the town of Alba – thus the sobriquet, 'Alba truffle'. Less perfumed white truffles are found elsewhere in Italy, even as far south as Calabria. The white truffle looks like a potato, usually around 50g (1¾oz) in weight (although it can be much bigger), and it grows in symbiosis with oak, hazel, poplar and beech trees. The flesh is solid, brittle and highly perfumed. The Italians use white truffles very thinly sliced or grated as a scent on a dish of food – on pasta, for instance, or a plate of superb raw beef. I sometimes store them in the fridge with eggs, and the eggs become imbued with their scent, making *wonderful* scrambled eggs! White truffles can only be found by chance (today by dogs, formerly by female pigs), as they cannot be cultivated. This is why they are the most sought-after treasure, achieving the price of £3,000–£4,000 per kilogram ($2,000–$2,500 per pound)!

The French love their black **Périgord truffle** (*Tuber melanosporum*, or *tartufo nero* or *tartufo invernale*), and because it is the only truffle to appear in France, believe it is the best. It grows in the Périgord, obviously, but is also found in Provence, and in Italy too, in Umbria and Norcia (in the Marches), and elsewhere throughout the world. It grows in symbiosis with oak trees. The subterranean fruit body is black, with a rough skin, and the insides are wonderfully perfumed. The French use their truffles slightly differently, often storing them in a jar of oil or duck fat, which then becomes wonderfully fragranced. They sliver them as well with potato and egg dishes, and in salads. Slivers of truffle are wonderful under the skin of a roast chicken or turkey.

*T. melanosporum* can be cultivated, and in many places the roots of young oaks have been treated with truffle spores before planting. In New Zealand, for instance, they successfully cultivate black truffles in former grape-vine plantations. I was the patron of a truffle festival in Australia, where a friend of mine, Peter Marshall, planted a few hundred hazel trees some fifteen years ago, the roots of which were impregnated with the spores of *T. melanosporum*. He now enjoys a very satisfactory production of truffles in Eastern Australia. It was fantastic to watch the two trained dogs very quickly locating where truffles were growing, just a few centimetres beneath the earth. The dogs were happy to receive a piece of sausage as a reward, while Peter and his family were over the moon collecting kilos and kilos of what is commonly called the 'Black Diamond'.

The **summer truffle** (*T. aestivum*, or *scorzone*) can be found in many places, including England. It grows in symbiosis with a number of trees, usually oak, and is warty in appearance, rather like the black truffle. Its perfume is much more delicate.

# STRUDEL DI FUNGHI
*Mushroom Strudel*

When I was a student, I spent the most wonderful time in Vienna where I studied, but was also on the search for new foods and food specialities. I was impressed by the apple strudel, which the Viennese bake in a masterly way, and it was only years later that I had the idea of producing a savoury strudel filled with mushrooms. The result is very good indeed.

Preheat the oven to 200°C (400°F/gas 6).

You will want twelve pieces of filo altogether, so count the filo sheets in your packet, and cut if necessary to make twelve. Take three pieces of filo pastry at a time, and brush each sheet with melted butter. Then place on top of each other. Make four such piles, each consisting of three sheets of filo.

Now prepare the filling. Cook the onion in the butter until soft, about 10 minutes, then add the mushrooms with the nutmeg and stir-fry for 3–4 minutes. Add the sherry and let the alcohol evaporate a little over the heat, then stir in the cornflour, marjoram leaves and some salt and pepper to taste. Stir well and leave to cool.

Grease a large baking sheet with butter and line it with baking parchment, then lay on it, one at a time, the four separate piles of filo pastry. Brush the edges with beaten egg, and put a quarter of the mushroom mixture in the centre of each pile. Before folding them up, add about a quarter of the Parmesan to each pile. Close the piles of filo by rolling them up. Moisten the join with beaten egg, close firmly, then place each pile of rolled filo, join-down, on the baking sheet. Brush the beaten egg over all the exposed pastry.

Bake in the preheated oven for 15 minutes. Cut the strudels in half if you are serving to more than four people for a starter, otherwise serve each person one whole strudel.

SERVES 4–6 AS A STARTER

—200g (7oz) filo pastry
—60g (2¼oz) unsalted butter, melted
—1 medium egg, beaten, for wash

FILLING
—1 medium onion, peeled and
    finely chopped
—40g (1½oz) unsalted butter
—500g (1lb 2oz) wild and cultivated
    mushrooms, cleaned weight
—freshly grated nutmeg
—1 tablespoon dry sherry
—1 tablespoon cornflour (cornstarch)
—leaves from 1 sprig of fresh marjoram
—30g (1oz) Parmesan, freshly grated
—salt and freshly ground black pepper

*cultivated mushrooms*

# FRITTO MISTO DI FUNGHI
*Mixed Mushroom Fritters*

The Italians like fried stuff. In Piedmont there is a *fritto misto* made from at least thirteen different types of vegetables and meat. Anything that can be sliced, breadcrumbed and fried is welcome, including mushrooms. For this particular *fritto*, however, it is nice to have bigger-sized mushrooms, and the Italians use mostly ceps or *porcini* for this. But a good mixture of mushrooms, wild and cultivated, will do very well indeed, using chestnuts, brown caps, even Portobello.

Wipe the mushroom caps, then cut them into slices about 6–7mm (about ⅜ inch) thick. Dust the slices with flour, then dip them into the egg, then into the breadcrumbs.

Heat the olive oil until hot, and fry the mushroom slices, turning when one side is brown. It will only take a few minutes. Drain on absorbent kitchen paper and serve hot, seasoned with salt and pepper, with a wedge of lemon.

SERVES 4

—4 large mushroom caps (Portobello), about 600–700g (1lb 5oz–1lb 9oz), cleaned weight
—plain flour (all-purpose flour), for dusting
—1 large egg, beaten
—80g (2¾oz / about ¾ cup) dried white breadcrumbs
—about 5 tablespoons extra virgin olive oil
—salt and freshly ground black pepper
—2 lemons, halved

# FUNGHI CON POLENTA
*Polenta with Mushrooms*

A classic of Italian food, polenta and mushrooms. *Porcini* are the favourite, in the autumn, in risotto, with pasta or with polenta as here, and if you have them, do use them. But if you can't find them, use the delicious brown cap mushrooms from the supermarket, perhaps with the addition of some dried *funghi porcini,* for more flavour. In season, you'll find this recipe served in every second restaurant in little villages in the mountains.

Wipe the mushrooms with a damp cloth, and slice. Please do not peel. Finely chop the drained *funghi porcini.* (Save the water for soup, it is full of flavour.)

Heat the olive oil in a large pan and add the garlic, the sliced mushrooms and the chopped *funghi porcini.* Sauté for about 5–10 minutes, very gently. Add the tomatoes, season to taste with salt and pepper, and cook for about 10–15 minutes.

Meanwhile, cook the polenta until soft and hot. Divide between individual plates, put the mushroom sauce to the side, and sprinkle with the Parmesan.

SERVES 4

—1 recipe *polenta concia* (see page 211)
—40g (1¹/₂oz) Parmesan, freshly grated

SAUCE
—300g (10¹/₂oz) fresh and firm brown cap mushrooms
—10g (¹/₄oz) dried ceps (*funghi porcini*), soaked in hot water for 20–30 minutes, drained
—4 tablespoons extra virgin olive oil
—2 garlic cloves, peeled and chopped
—1 x 400g (14oz) tin of chopped tomatoes
—salt and freshly ground black pepper

# FILLETI DI SOGLIOLA CON FINFERLI
*Fillet of Dover Sole with Chanterelles*

I am very pleased to live in England because it has so many wonderful food ingredients, one of them being Dover sole, probably one of the best fish you can eat. I usually have it *meunière*, dusted with flour and cooked in butter until brown, and I particularly like the crispy edges. I also like to bone the fish myself, which is half the fun.

Sole and chanterelles are complementary, but the combination, I have to admit, is pure decadence.

—2 large Dover sole
—plain flour (all-purpose flour), for dusting
—100g (3½oz) unsalted butter
—2 spring onions (scallions), very finely chopped
—250g (9oz) fresh chanterelles, cleaned weight
—salt and freshly ground black pepper

Clean and fillet the fish, and skin them on both sides – or get your fishmonger to do this. You will have four fillets. Dip them in flour. Melt half the butter in a large frying pan and cook the fillets very gently, not too hot, for about 8 minutes on each side, until brown. You may have to do this in batches, or use two frying pans. Add salt and pepper to taste, and keep warm.

Meanwhile, in another frying pan, melt the rest of the butter, and fry the spring onions for a few minutes. Add the chanterelles, and fry for another 8 minutes. Season with salt and pepper, and then serve the fish fillets on warm plates, accompanied by the chanterelles. Enjoy.

**SERVES 4**

*wild mushrooms*

# FUNGHI MISTI SALTATI
*Mixed Sautéed Mushrooms*

I invariably end up cooking this recipe when I come back from collecting mushrooms, when there are a few different types to bring together. For a moment I wonder, should I turn them into a soup, should I fry them as fritters? No, I make a lovely mixed sauté, which I sometimes eat on toast, or serve with polenta. The only thing I know for certain is that they are delicious.

Heat the butter or olive oil in a large frying pan, then add the garlic and fry extremely gently, just to soften it, for 5 minutes or so. Add the mushrooms and stir-fry for another 5 or so minutes. I prefer them a little *al dente*, so I don't cook them until soft. Add salt and pepper at the end, and the parsley.

Serve on the *bruschetta*. Eat warm.

SERVES 4–6

—50g (1¾oz) unsalted butter or 3 tablespoons extra virgin olive oil
—2 large garlic cloves, peeled and crushed
—500g (1lb 2oz) mixed wild mushrooms, cleaned weight, plus some cultivated, if your search hasn't been too successful
—2 tablespoons finely chopped fresh flat-leaf parsley
—salt and freshly ground black pepper

TO SERVE
—4–6 slices *bruschetta* (see page 119)

# MEDAGLIONI DI CERVO CON MORCHELLE
*Venison Medallions with Morels*

The greatest combination of wild food for me is game and morels, and here I have chosen venison fillet. Morels are not easy to find in the wild, but you can buy them dried, usually coming from Nepal, Tibet or Turkey. When rehydrated in water, they assume the same size as the original. When I clean them, after soaking, I take care that there are no strange little stones or the like: this mushroom has the peculiarity of collecting things inside its elongated cap, as it is hollow.

I like to serve this with truffled potato purée (see page 111), which makes it a dish for kings.

Cut the venison fillet carefully into medallions: you want three medallions per person (twelve in all), each about 30–35g (1–1¼oz) in weight.

Drain the morels, and check them for impurities. Heat the butter in a medium frying pan, and fry the spring onions and the morels for 5–6 minutes.

Meanwhile, coat the medallions with plain flour. Heat the olive oil in another medium pan and fry the medallions with the sage leaves until the meat starts to brown, no more than 2 minutes each side. Set aside on a plate.

Continue with the morels, adding the brandy and balsamic vinegar, and some salt and pepper to taste.

Now add the medallions and sage to the morel pan. Quickly deglaze the venison pan with a little stock, bringing it to the boil and scraping up any tasty bits. Add this liquid to the morels, and taste and adjust the seasoning if necessary. Serve immediately.

SERVES 4

—about 450g (1lb) venison fillet, in the piece
—30g (1oz) dried morels, soaked in warm water for 30 minutes
—50g (1¾oz) unsalted butter
—2 spring onions (scallions), chopped
—a little plain flour (all-purpose flour), for coating
—4 tablespoons extra virgin olive oil
—8 fresh sage leaves
—2 tablespoons brandy
—1 tablespoon old balsamic vinegar
—a little meat or chicken stock as required
—salt and freshly ground black pepper

*wild mushrooms*

# ZUPPA DI FUNGHI MISTI
*Wild Mushroom Soup*

This is a very delightful soup, which I like best with lots of texture, so I don't blend it. I make it usually with a mixture of wild mushrooms, but you can also make it with a mix of cultivated ones plus a little dried *funghi porcini* for flavour. Whether wild or cultivated, this soup is warm, comforting and makes a lovely starter.

Finely slice the cleaned mushrooms. Chop the drained *funghi porcini*.

Heat the olive oil in a large saucepan and fry the onion for 10 minutes, until soft. Add the sliced mushrooms and the chopped *funghi porcini*, and fry for about 8 minutes. Then add the cornflour and stock, with the *porcini* soaking water, and mix well together. Simmer for about 30 minutes. Taste for seasoning.

Should you prefer a creamy soup, blend it in a food processor. (You could perhaps add a couple of tablespoons of double cream/heavy cream.)

Serve sprinkled with the parsley and Parmesan.

SERVES 4

—300g (10½oz) mixed wild and cultivated mushrooms, cleaned weight
—10g (¼oz) dried ceps (*funghi porcini*), soaked in hot water for 20–30 minutes, drained (save the water)
—4 tablespoons extra virgin olive oil
—1 onion, peeled and finely sliced
—½ tablespoon cornflour (cornstarch)
—1.5 litres (2¾ pints/6 cups) chicken or vegetable stock
—2 tablespoons finely chopped fresh flat-leaf parsley
—50g (1¾oz) Parmesan, freshly grated
—salt and freshly ground black pepper

# TAGLIOLINI CON GALLETTI E ANIMELLE
*Tagliolini with Chanterelles and Sweetbreads*

*Tagliolini* is the smallest shape of *tagliatelle*, which is often made by hand with egg pasta. Because of its delicate taste it is usually combined with truffle, chicken livers or delicate seafood. Here I have chosen subtle veal sweetbreads, with the glowing yellow of chanterelles.

Cook the sauce first. Plunge the sweetbreads into boiling salted water for 2 minutes, then leave to cool. Remove and discard all the outer sinews, and chop the flesh into small ribbons.

Heat the olive oil and butter together in a large pan and sauté the onion for 10 minutes. Add the chopped *funghi porcini*, the sweetbreads and wine, and stir-fry for 5 minutes. Add the chanterelles and parsley, and cook for another 5 minutes, adding a little of the *porcini* soaking water for extra moisture. Season with salt and pepper to taste.

Cook the pasta in plenty of salted water until *al dente*, then drain and mix with the sauce. Serve on hot plates, with the Parmesan sprinkled on top.

SERVES 4

—300g (10½oz) fresh *tagliolini* pasta (or 250g/9oz dried)
—20g (¾oz) Parmesan, freshly grated

SAUCE
—300g (10½oz) veal sweetbreads
—3 tablespoons extra virgin olive oil
—25g (1oz) unsalted butter
—1 small onion, peeled and very finely chopped
—10g (¼oz) dried ceps (*funghi porcini*), soaked in hot water for 20–30 minutes, drained and chopped (save a little of the water)
—125ml (4fl oz/½ cup) dry white wine
—200g (7oz) chanterelles, cleaned weight, roughly chopped
—2 tablespoons finely chopped fresh flat-leaf parsley
—salt and freshly ground black pepper

# UOVA IN TEGAME CON TARTUFO NERO
*Baked Eggs with Black Truffle*

Every year this is my little Christmas indulgence, baked eggs with truffles. The season of the black truffle is from around September through to February. It is not as intense in flavour as the white truffle, but it is delightful, and is not nearly as expensive as the white one – which is some sort of consolation. Should you be able to invest in a black truffle, shave it on top of the ramekin before serving. Lacking the real thing, you can use truffle butter and truffle oil, which you will find in delicatessens.

Preheat the oven to 200°C (400°F/gas 6).

Grease four 7.5cm (3 inch) ramekins with truffle butter, then crack in the eggs. Pour in the cream, then put into the preheated oven for about 6–7 minutes, or until you see that the white of the eggs have solidified, but the yolks are still runny.

Take the ramekins out of the oven, pour a few drops of truffle oil on the top, and serve. It's a great breakfast, or a lavish first course.

SERVES 4

**PER PERSON**
—½ tablespoon truffle butter
—2 medium eggs
—3 tablespoons double cream (heavy cream)
—a few drops of truffle oil

# CARNE ALL'ALBESE CON MAGNATUM
## *Raw Beef Salad with Truffle*

This is a very typically Piedmontese recipe, based on the white truffle, the prize of Alba. This very elusive fungus, which grows underground in only a few parts of the world (not just Italy), can cost up to £3,000 per kilogram ($2,000 per pound). You need only a very small amount to flavour any food.

At the end of 2015, I did a television series in Australia, where I devised a *carpaccio* made with fillet of kangaroo. I was missing the truffle there, but the combination would have been perfect.

Place the beef medallions on a piece of baking paper, top with another piece of paper, then beat until very flat.

Divide the flattened medallions between individual plates. Add a few drops of truffle oil, extra virgin olive oil and lemon juice. Shave a little truffle over the top, and add salt and pepper to taste. To be eaten with good toasted bread, as a wonderful starter.

SERVES 4

—280g (10oz) fillet of beef, cut into 12 slices or medallions
—a few drops of truffle oil
—2 tablespoons extra virgin olive oil
—juice of 1 lemon
—as much white truffle as you can afford!
—salt and freshly ground black pepper

# REGIONS OF ITALY

1. PIEDMONT
2. VAL D'AOSTA
3. LOMBARDY
4. TRENTINO-ALTO ADIGE
5. VENETO
6. FRULI-VENEZIA GIULIA
7. LIGURIA
8. EMILIA-ROMAGNA
9. TUSCANY
10. UMBRIA
11. MARCHE
12. LAZIO
13. ABRUZZO
14. MOLISE
15. CAMPANIA
16. PUGLIA
17. BASILICATA
18. CALABRIA
19. SICILY
20. SARDINIA

Most of the recipes included in this book are accompanied by a map of Italy showing the region from where the recipe hails, which is highlighted in a darker shade of green. The larger map of Italy on this page shows all these regions, with a key above. For the recipes that are not accompanied by a map of Italy, this is because they do not originate from any one particular Italian region.

Italian food is distinctly regional, partly because the country was only united politically in 1861. Before then it comprised of disparate (often warring) regions, states and cities, all of which differed marginally, sometimes radically, from their neighbours, in customs, politics, and in styles of food and cooking. But it is the geography that played, and still plays, the most determining role in defining culinary styles. Italy has no less than 1,500 miles of coastline and seafood is obviously more important to those regions that abut the Adriatic and Mediterranean than to those which are landlocked. Italy is almost entirely composed of mountains – the Apennine range which forms the country's backbone, stretching from Piedmont in the north right down to Calabria in the south. In the mountains basic ingredients are unlike those of the coastal plains, and the basic style of cookery differs as a result. The sheer length of the country, from the Alpine north down to the 'toe' of the Italian 'boot', dictates that styles differ radically – that of the north being more Germanic, cold-weather cooking characterised by the use of butter; that of the sun-baked south, more Mediterranean, often veering towards its sunny neighbours in Greece and North Africa where olive oil is the main ingredient used for cooking.

# INDEX

Publishing director: Sarah Lavelle
Project editor: Laura Herring
Editor: Susan Fleming
Creative director: Helen Lewis
Design and art direction: Claire Rochford
Photographer: Laura Edwards
Photographer's assistant: Kendal Noctor
Food stylists: Anna Jones, Emily Ezekiel
Food stylists' assistants: Anna Barnett,
Chrissie Chung
Illustrator: Katie Horwich
Production Director: Vincent Smith
Production Controller: Tom Moore

First published in 2016 by
Quadrille Publishing
Pentagon House
52–54 Southwark Street
London SE1 1UN
www.quadrille.co.uk
www.quadrille.com

Quadrille is an imprint of Hardie Grant
www.hardiegrant.com.au

Text © 2016 Quadrille Publishing
Photography © 2016 Laura Edwards
Illustration © 2016 Katie Horwich
Design and layout © 2016 Quadrille Publishing

Cataloguing in Publication Data: a catalogue record for this book is
available from the British Library.

ISBN: 978 184949 752 7

Printed in China